TRIUMPHAL PROCESSION. (See the note on l. 665.)
Relief from the Arch of Titus (about 82 A.D.) in the Roman Forum.

SELECTIONS FROM
FIVE ROMAN AUTHORS

Also available:

First Book of Latin Poetry, H. Flewett & W. Pantin
Four Greek Authors, E. Kennedy
Selections from Five Roman Poets, H. Gould & J. Whiteley
Two Centuries of Roman Poetry, E. Kennedy & A. Davis
Two Centuries of Roman Prose, E. Kennedy & A. Davis

SELECTIONS FROM
FIVE ROMAN AUTHORS

(NEPOS, CAESAR, SALLUST, LIVY, CICERO)

Edited with Introduction,
Notes and Vocabulary by
H.E. GOULD
and
J.L. WHITELEY

Bristol Classical Press

First published by Macmillan Education Ltd in 1942

This edition published in 1997 by
Bristol Classical Press
an imprint of
Gerald Duckworth & Co. Ltd
The Old Piano Factory
48 Hoxton Square, London N1 6PB

Reprinted 1998

A catalogue record for this book is available
from the British Library

ISBN 1-85399-531-2

Available in USA and Canada from:
Focus Information Group
PO Box 369
Newburyport
MA 01950

Printed in Great Britain by
Booksprint, Bristol

CONTENTS

LIST OF ILLUSTRATIONS

MAPS

INTRODUCTION

THE five authors who are represented in this volume of selections from their works, all lived in the first century B.C., a period of great importance in the history of the Roman Empire, for it was during this century that the Roman World almost collapsed owing to the failure of the Roman Republic to maintain order and a stable form of government. Fortunately the genius of Julius Caesar and the wise statesmanship of his relative and successor Augustus laid the foundations of the Principate which gave stability and security to the Mediterranean for another four centuries.

Of our five authors, three of them, Caesar, Cicero, and Sallust, played important parts in the history of the period, so that for a proper understanding of their work, it will be necessary briefly to describe the course of events during this century and the momentous issues that were at stake.

Theoretically, the Roman Republic was democratic in its working, and during the earlier years of Rome's history, it had worked efficiently and smoothly in the administration of a city-state and the adjoining territory. As Rome's power grew, however, and she became, first, the ruler of Italy, and later, by the first century B.C., the mistress of the Mediterranean world, the constitution which had served the city of Rome well, proved unequal to solving the new problems which presented themselves. Moreover, owing to a variety of causes, the Republican constitution itself ceased to be truly democratic, for all the real power became concentrated in the hands of a few families, identified with the senate, which at this time not only lacked statesmen who had the vision or the courage to grapple with the new problems, but also was filled with members who were concerned chiefly with retaining the reins of government to the exclusion of all others.

A generation before Caesar's and Cicero's birth, in 133 and 123 B.C., the political supremacy of the senate was temporarily shaken by two ardent reformers, the Gracchi brothers, Tiberius and Gaius, who seem to have made an honest attempt to solve several serious problems, such as unemployment, the disappearance of the small farmer, and the relations between Rome and her allies in Italy. The senate put every obstacle in their path, and eventually the Gracchi lost their lives in street fighting and the senatorial order quickly re-established its supremacy.

In the first century B.C., a new and grim figure appeared on the Roman political stage, the successful general at the head of the now professional army, whose power the senate failed completely to control.[1] Thus when class warfare broke out again, and both the senate and the popular party, as the reformers were now called, openly resorted to force, both sides looked for support to the outstanding general of the day who could get bills passed with the aid of his troops. Thus civil war broke out, and it was characterised by cruelty and massacre on both sides.

For example, during the second decade of the first century, when Caesar and Cicero were quite young men, there were three civil wars, and Rome was twice besieged and captured by Roman generals in command of Roman and Italian troops. More horrible still, in 80 B.C., Sulla began the system of 'proscriptions', under which all those whose political opinions were regarded as dangerous to the winning side could be killed with impunity.

The next twenty years, 80–60 B.C., were momentous in the history of the Roman Republic. Sulla's attempts to bolster up the power of the senate gradually collapsed before attacks from several

---

[1] Unless he happened to support the senatorial government, as did Sulla.

quarters, especially from Pompey and Caesar, the latter of whom was beginning to take an active part in politics and held a succession of magistracies, becoming quaestor in 68 B.C., aedile in 65, praetor in 62, and, in 61 governor, as propraetor, of Further Spain, where he gained some minor successes over the natives of what is now Portugal.

During the same period, Cicero had first established his reputation as a lawyer and an orator, and then had entered political life, becoming aedile in 69 B.C., praetor in 66 and consul in 63 B.C. His consular year of office will always be remembered for the vigorous way in which he crushed a dangerous attempt at a *coup d'état* on the part of Catiline, an unscrupulous noble who hoped to rally to his side the many discontented elements in Italy. The fact that there was so much dissatisfaction in the country is a strong indictment of the senatorial government of the preceding seventy years.

By this time the failure of the senate to maintain order and a strong, stable government was becoming apparent even to the most die-hard supporters of that party. Cicero, himself a loyal partisan, realising that something must be done, if the Roman world was not to dissolve in chaos, attempted to form a strong government, capable of maintaining order in Rome and the provinces, and of controlling the

recklessness of demagogic tribunes and their irre-
sponsible followers among the landless and workless
mob in Rome.   He aimed at establishing a kind of
' National Government ', a combination not only of
senators, business men and financiers, but also of the
upper classes in the Italian cities, to be protected
by a loyal general and a strong force of troops.   He
cast Pompey for the role of protector of the constitution.

Such an ideal, however, failed to work.   In the
first place, in 60 B.C., the alliance between Caesar,
Pompey and Crassus, known as the First Triumvirate,[1] showed that the senate had now lost all
power of independent action.   Secondly, there was
Julius Caesar to be reckoned with, an ambitious man
who gradually came to realise that the Roman
Republic was too far gone for remedial treatment,
and should be replaced by a new system.

The results of the First Triumvirate were not
immediately apparent.   But Caesar obtained a
provincial command and the opportunity to create
an army, without which he realised he could do
nothing.   He was appointed governor of Cisalpine
Gaul (the Po valley), Illyricum (north-east shores of

[1] Apparently Caesar wished to win Cicero's support for
the Triumvirate, but Caesar's unconstitutional attitude
made the orator stand aloof.

the Adriatic) and Transalpine Gaul (South-east France).

While Caesar was absent in Gaul from 58–49 B.C., and adding to the Roman Empire the new and rich province of Gaul, constitutional government in Rome itself broke down and anarchy became widespread, as is well illustrated by the careers of Milo and Clodius. In 53 B.C., these two men were candidates for the consulship and praetorship respectively, and each maintained a gang of gladiators who engaged in numerous fights in the streets and made it unsafe for peaceful citizens to go abroad.

The extract in this book from Cicero's speech in defence of Milo (*Pro Milone*) relates how the two rivals met on the Appian Way and Clodius was slain in the ensuing scuffle. The riots that attended the latter's funeral were so serious that the senate had to invite the aid of Pompey and his troops to maintain order.

In 52 B.C., Sallust, another of our authors, became tribune, and joining the popular party, showed bitter hostility to Milo. The latter was condemned and had to go into exile.

During these years, the triumvirate continued to exist, but only precariously. At one time in 56 B.C. it almost collapsed, but the three partners held a conference, patched up their quarrels and made arrangements for the future : among them, Caesar's command was prolonged, and Crassus and Pompey also gained military positions. But after Crassus was killed fighting in the East, a second and severer crisis arose in which the senate succeeded in alienating Pompey from Caesar, and in 49 B.C. civil war broke out between Caesar and the senate, the latter led by Pompey.

It took Caesar four years to crush the senatorial party in Spain, Greece, North Africa,[1] and finally in Spain. By 45 B.C. he was virtually the sole ruler of the Roman Empire. A year later, he was assassinated by a group of senators, led by Brutus, who seems to have honestly believed that, with Caesar removed, the Roman Republic would be restored in its original form.

If we are to understand Cicero's feeling at this time, his distress at his exile[2] in 58 B.C., his unrestrained joy at his recall the following year, his dismay at the dictatorial position of Julius Caesar, and his delight at his murder, we have to remember that to Cicero, a political career in what he considered a free state with democratic forms of government,

[1] Sallust accompanied Caesar in his African campaign and was appointed by him governor of Numidia.

[2] Engineered by Clodius, his bitter personal enemy, and supported by Caesar after his proposals of alliance had been rebuffed.

was the only legitimate career for a free man. He could never forget that he himself had risen to the top and won the consulship and a seat in the senate by his own ability and merit. He failed to see, as Caesar saw clearly enough, that the Republic was past mending. Thus, after Caesar's murder, Cicero attempted once more to form a ' National Government ', only to fail yet again. Moreover, he embittered Antony, Caesar's successor, and eventually was slain.

The Republic did not long survive him, for after another period of civil war, Octavian, grand-nephew of Julius Caesar and his heir, defeated Antony and became supreme master of the Roman world, and, as Augustus, the first Roman emperor, founder of the Roman Principate.

NOTES ON NEPOS, CAESAR, SALLUST, LIVY AND CICERO

Little is known of our first author, NEPOS (c. 100–25 B.C.) except that he spent most of his life in Rome, devoted himself to literature, wrote a number of historical works which are now lost, and was a friend of Cicero and Atticus. All we possess of his works are twenty-four biographies of famous men, most of them Greeks, but with two Romans among them (Cato and Atticus, the correspondent of Cicero).

His Latin is straightforward and readily understood and so makes him an excellent introduction to Latin prose. But his style is poor and dull, while his method of dealing with the subjects of his biographies is not only prosaic, but lacks colour and historical appreciation.

CAESAR's contribution to Latin literature consists of his commentaries or notes for the history of his Gallic campaigns and of the Civil War with Pompey and the senate,—works which have been school text books for centuries. The chief aim of these notes is not primarily to record facts, but to put forward their author in the most favourable light, to illustrate his great services to the state and the empire, and to emphasise his own moderation and clemency, qualities that he undoubtedly possessed. This is not to say that much of Caesar's work is fiction. On the contrary, most of it is undoubtedly true, but by skilful arrangement and discreet omission, Caesar sought to popularise his own achievements and to throw the responsibility for the Civil War on Pompey and the senate.

SALLUST, our third author (86–35 B.C.), took an active part in the political life of the period, without, however, any noteworthy distinction. After he had returned to Rome from his post as governor of N. Africa, he seems to have devoted himself to a leisurely and elegant retirement during which he wrote two monographs, ' The Conspiracy of Catiline ', ' The War against Jugurtha ', and a history of the period 78–67 B.C. Only fragments survive from the history, but we possess the two monographs complete.

The political sympathies of Sallust (he was a Caesarian) are apparent in both the *Catiline* and the *Jugurtha*. In the former, he describes the attempted *coup d'état* of the bankrupt aristocrat and indirectly praises the work and political leadership of Caesar, at the same time damning Cicero with faint praise. In the latter, he describes the Roman campaigns in N. Africa against the upstart prince Jugurtha. This war had been shockingly mismanaged by a series of corrupt and inefficient senatorial nominees, and brought to a successful conclusion only by the energy and vigour of a plebeian, Marius. In thus lauding the latter, whose memory had always remained popular with the democratic and Caesarian party, Sallust was again true to his political convictions or prejudices. It is interesting to note how he represents Sulla, a noble, as a cunning and unscrupulous demagogue.

His style is consciously archaic, concise, compressed, yet at the same time rhetorical and eloquent. He is at his best in describing vigorous action. All these qualities are clearly illustrated in the passage which has been included in this volume, viz., the closing chapters of his *War against Jugurtha*, which describe the treacherous surrender of the Numidian prince to Sulla, Marius' quaestor.

LIVY (59 B.C.–A.D. 17) took no part in public affairs, but seems to have devoted himself to his great work, the history of Rome from the foundation of the city until his own day.

The first instalments of his history appeared between 27 and 25 B.C., and brought him an immediate and lasting fame which was further increased by the later instalments.

Of the 142 books we now possess only 1–10, and 21–45, but we have short abstracts of the contents of them all.

We should be foolish to expect of ancient historians the exactitude, philosophical attitude, and patient research which are now demanded of modern historians. In any case, as he tells us in his preface, Livy sought to commemorate the deeds and heroes which had made Rome great, and to idealise the old Roman virtues of honour, probity, and devotion to the state.

Livy's power of graphic description, and his keen sense of the dramatic, are fully illustrated in the examples that have been chosen from his works,

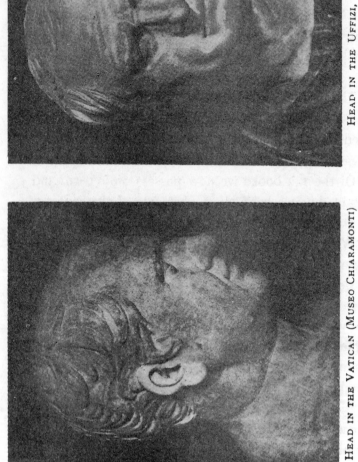

HEAD IN THE VATICAN (MUSEO CHIARAMONTI)　　HEAD IN THE UFFIZI, FLORENCE

These two heads are generally, but not certainly, identified with
Marcus Tullius Cicero.

in the magnificent stories, ' How Horatius kept the Bridge ', ' Mucius Scaevola ', and ' the Gauls March on Rome '.

The political life of CICERO has already been discussed in the general introduction. Now it remains for us to consider his literary career.

His works may be divided into three groups : (i) his speeches, both legal and political, which reveal him as the undisputed master of Roman eloquence ; (ii) his voluminous correspondence, which not only gives us a vivid and varied picture of Roman political and social life during the last days of the Roman Republic, but also reveals to us Cicero's nature and character, impressionable, irresolute and exceedingly vain, yet at the same time intelligent, honourable, and affectionate; and finally (iii) his philosophical works, which he began to write with ever increasing devotion and interest after his retirement from politics. In these works, most of which he composed during three memorable years, 46–44 B.C., Cicero not only sought relief from the lamentable Civil War, but also aimed at explaining and criticising for the benefit of educated Romans, the doctrines and tenets of the leading Greek philosophical schools. Under (iii) we may classify two charming essays on ' Old Age ' and ' Friendship '

This volume contains a selection from his speech on behalf of Milo (*Pro Milone*), a chapter from his essay 'On Friendship' and one of the many letters which he wrote to his great friend Atticus.

NEPOS (Cornelius Nepos)

Historian (contemporary and friend of Cicero)

The Rise and Fall of Miltiades, the Athenian General and Statesman

3. Eisdem temporibus Persarum rex Darius ex
Asia in Europam exercitu traiecto Scythis bellum
inferre decrevit. Pontem fecit in Histro flumine,
qua copias traduceret : eius pontis, dum ipse
abesset, custodes reliquit principes, quos secum ex 5
Ionia et Aeolide duxerat ; quibus singulis ipsarum
urbium perpetua dederat imperia. Sic enim facillime putavit se Graeca lingua loquentes qui Asiam
incolerent, sub sua retenturum potestate, si amicis
suis oppida tuenda tradidisset, quibus se oppresso 10
nulla spes salutis relinqueretur. In hoc fuit tum
numero Miltiades, cui illa custodia crederetur. Hic
cum crebri adferrent nuntii male rem gerere Darium
premique a Scythis, Miltiades hortatus est pontis
custodes ne a fortuna datam occasionem liberandae 15
Graeciae dimitterent : nam si cum his copiis quas
secum transportarat interisset Darius, non solum
Europam fore tutam, sed etiam eos qui Asiam incolerent Graeci genere, liberos a Persarum futuros

20 dominatione et periculo : et facile effici posse ;
ponte enim rescisso, regem vel hostium ferro vel
inopia paucis diebus interiturum : ad hoc consilium
cum plerique accederent, Histiaeus Milesius ne res
conficeretur obstitit, dicens non idem ipsis qui
25 summas imperii tenerent, expedire et multitudini,
quod Darii regno ipsorum niteretur dominatio ;
quo exstincto, ipsos potestate expulsos civibus suis
poenas daturos : itaque adeo se abhorrere a ceter-
orum consilio, ut nihil putet ipsis utilius quam con-
30 firmari regnum Persarum. Huius cum sententiam
plurimi essent secuti, Miltiades, non dubitans tam
multis consciis ad regis aures consilia sua per-
ventura, Chersonesum reliquit ac rursus Athenas
demigravit. Cuius ratio etsi non valuit, tamen
35 magnopere est laudanda, cum amicior omnium
libertati quam suae fuerit dominationi.

4. Darius autem cum ex Europa in Asiam
redisset, hortantibus amicis ut Graeciam redigeret
in suam potestatem, classem quingentarum navium
40 comparavit, eique Datim praefecit et Artaphernem,
hisque ducenta peditum decem milia equitum
dedit, causam interserens se hostem esse Atheniensibus, quod eorum auxilio Iones Sardes expugnassent
suaque praesidia interfecissent. Illi praefecti regii,
45 classe ad Euboeam appulsa, celeriter Eretriam
ceperunt, omnesque eius gentis cives abreptos in

Asiam ad regem miserunt. Inde ad Atticam accesserunt ac suas copias in campum Marathona deduxerunt : is est ab oppido circiter milia passuum decem. Hoc tumultu Athenienses tam propinquo 50 tamque magno permoti auxilium nusquam nisi a Lacedaemoniis petiverunt, Philippidemque cursorem eius generis, qui hemerodromoe vocantur, Lacedaemonem miserunt, ut nuntiaret quam celeri opus esset auxilio. Domi autem creant decem praetores 55 qui exercitui praeessent, in eis Miltiadem : inter quos magna fuit contentio, utrum moenibus se defenderent an obviam irent hostibus acieque decernerent. Unus Miltiades maxime nitebatur ut primo quoque tempore castra fierent : id si factum 60 esset, et civibus animum accessurum, cum viderent de eorum virtute non desperari, et hostes eadem re fore tardiores, si animadverterent auderi adversus se tam exiguis copiis dimicare.

5. Hoc in tempore nulla civitas Atheniensibus 65 auxilio fuit praeter Plataeenses : ea mille misit milites : itaque horum adventu decem milia armatorum completa sunt ; quae manus mirabili flagrabat pugnandi cupiditate : quo factum est ut plus quam collegae Miltiades valeret. Eius ergo 70 auctoritate impulsi Athenienses copias ex urbe eduxerunt locoque idoneo castra fecerunt. Dein postero die sub montis radicibus acie regione

instructa non apertissima proelium commiserunt:
75 namque arbores multis locis erant rarae, hoc
consilio, ut et montium altitudine tegerentur et
arborum tractu equitatus hostium impediretur, ne
multitudine clauderentur. Datis, etsi non aequum
locum videbat suis, tamen fretus numero copiarum
80 suarum confligere cupiebat, eoque magis quod,
priusquam Lacedaemonii subsidio venirent, dimicare utile arbitrabatur: itaque in aciem peditum
centum equitum decem milia produxit, proeliumque
commisit. In quo tanto plus virtute valuerunt
85 Athenienses ut decemplicem numerum hostium
profligarint, adeoque eos perterruerint ut Persae
non castra sed naves petierint. Qua pugna nihil
adhuc exstitit nobilius: nulla enim unquam tam
exigua manus tantas opes prostravit.

90   6. Cuius victoriae non alienum videtur quale
praemium Miltiadi sit tributum docere, quo facilius
intellegi possit eandem omnium civitatum esse
naturam. Ut enim populi Romani honores quondam fuerunt rari et tenues, ob eamque causam
95 gloriosi, nunc autem effusi atque obsoleti, sic olim
apud Athenienses fuisse reperimus. Namque huic
Miltiadi, quia Athenas totamque Graeciam liberarat,
talis honos tributus est, in porticu, quae Poecile
vocatur, cum pugna depingeretur Marathonia, ut
100 in- decem praetorum numero prima eius imago

THE PLAIN OF MARATHON

from the foothills where the Athenian army took up its position. In the distance is the island of Euboea.

poneretur, isque hortaretur milites proeliumque
committeret : idem ille populus, posteaquam maius
imperium est nactus et largitione magistratuum
corruptus est, trecentas statuas Demetrio Phalereo
105 decrevit.

7. Post hoc proelium classem septuaginta navium
Athenienses eidem Miltiadi dederunt, ut insulas
quae barbaros adiuverant, bello persequeretur :
quo imperio plerasque ad officium redire coegit,
110 non nullas vi expugnavit. Ex his Parum insulam
opibus elatam cum oratione reconciliare non posset,
copias e navibus eduxit, urbem operibus clausit
omnique commeatu privavit ; dein vineis ac testudinibus constitutis propius muros accessit. Cum
115 iam in eo esset ut oppido potiretur, procul in continenti lucus, qui ex insula conspiciebatur, nescio
quo casu nocturno tempore incensus est : cuius
flamma ut ab oppidanis et oppugnatoribus est visa,
utrisque venit in opinionem, signum a classiariis
120 regis datum : quo factum est ut et Parii a deditione
deterrerentur, et Miltiades, timens ne classis regia
adventaret, incensis operibus quae statuerat, cum
totidem navibus atque erat profectus, Athenas
magna cum offensione civium suorum rediret.
125 Accusatus ergo est proditionis, quod, cum Parum
expugnare posset, a rege corruptus infectis rebus
discessisset. Eo tempore aeger erat vulneribus
quae in oppugnando oppido acceperat : itaque
quoniam ipse pro se dicere non posset, verba

fecit frater eius Stesagoras. Causa cognita capitis 130
absolutus pecunia multatus est ; eaque lis quinquaginta talentis aestimata est, quantus in classem
sumptus factus erat : hanc pecuniam quod solvere
in praesentia non poterat, in vincula publica
coniectus est ibique diem obiit supremum. 135

8. Hic etsi crimine Pario est accusatus, tamen
alia causa fuit damnationis : namque Athenienses
propter Pisistrati tyrannidem, quae paucis annis
ante fuerat, omnium civium suorum potentiam
extimescebant. Miltiades multum in imperiis mag- 140
nisque versatus non videbatur posse esse privatus,
praesertim cum consuetudine ad imperii cupiditatem
trahi videretur. Nam Chersonesi omnes illos quos
habitarat annos perpetuam obtinuerat domina-
tionem, tyrannusque fuerat appellatus, sed iustus : 145
non erat enim vi consecutus, sed suorum voluntate,
eamque potestatem bonitate retinebat : omnes
autem et dicuntur et habentur tyranni, qui potestate
sunt perpetua in ea civitate, quae libertate usa est.
Sed in Miltiade erat cum summa humanitas tum 150
mira communitas, ut nemo tam humilis esset, cui
non ad eum aditus pateret ; magna auctoritas
apud omnes civitates, nobile nomen, laus rei militaris maxima : haec populus respiciens maluit illum
innoxium plecti quam se diutius esse in timore. 155

(*Miltiades*, chapters 3–8.)

CAESAR (GAIUS JULIUS CAESAR)

Statesman, General and Historian, 101–43 B.C.

Curio in Africa

The citizens of Utica urge their governor, Varus, to surrender to the Caesarian army under Curio, but the news that King Juba is approaching with reinforcements restores their morale.

36. Postero die Curio Uticam obsidere et vallo circummunire instituit. Erat in oppido multitudo insolens belli diuturnitate otii, Uticenses pro quibusdam Caesaris in se beneficiis illi amicissimi, con-
160 ventus is qui ex variis generibus constaret, terror ex superioribus proeliis magnus. Itaque de deditione omnes palam loquebantur et cum P. Attio agebant, ne sua pertinacia omnium fortunas perturbari vellet. Haec cum agerentur, nuntii prae-
165 missi ab rege Iuba venerunt, qui illum cum magnis copiis adesse dicerent, et de custodia ac defensione urbis hortarentur. Quae res eorum perterritos animos confirmavit.

Convinced at last that the reports of the King's approach are true, Curio retires to Castra Cornelia, strengthens its defences and awaits reinforcements summoned from Sicily.

37. Nuntiabantur haec eadem Curioni, sed ali-
170 quamdiu fides fieri non poterat : tantam habebat

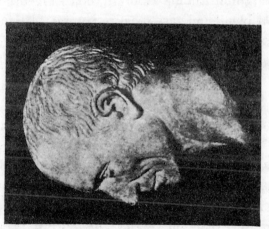

GAIUS JULIUS CAESAR

From the bust in the British Museum, the work of an Italian forger
of classical antiquities

suarum rerum fiduciam. Iamque Caesaris in Hispania res secundae in Africam nuntiis et litteris
perferebantur. Quibus rebus omnibus sublatus
nihil contra se regem ausurum existimabat. Sed
175 ubi certis auctoribus comperit minus XXV milibus
ab Utica eius copias abesse, relictis munitionibus
sese in castra Cornelia recepit. Huc frumentum
comportare, castra munire, materiam conferre coepit,
statimque in Siciliam misit uti II legiones reliquusque
180 equitatus ad se mitteretur. Castra erant ad bellum
ducendum aptissima natura loci et munitione et
maris propinquitate et aquae et salis copia, cuius
magna vis iam ex proximis erat salinis eo congesta.
Non materia multitudine arborum, non frumentum,
185 cuius erant plenissimi agri, deficere poterat. Itaque
omnium suorum consensu Curio reliquas copias
exspectare et bellum ducere parabat.

*Rashly crediting reports that the king has not left his territory,
and that only small Numidian forces are near, Curio
leaves his strong position. A night attack by his cavalry
meets with great success.*

38. His constitutis rebus probatisque consiliis,
ex perfugis quibusdam oppidanis audit Iubam
190 revocatum finitimo bello et controversiis Leptitanorum restitisse in regno ; Saburram, eius
praefectum, cum mediocribus copiis missum Uticae
appropinquare. His auctoribus temere credens con-

silium commutat et proelio rem committere constituit. Multum ad hanc rem probandam adiuvat 195
adulescentia, magnitudo animi, superioris temporis
proventus, fiducia rei bene gerendae. His rebus
impulsus equitatum omnem prima nocte ad castra
hostium mittit ad flumen Bagradam, quibus prae-
erat Saburra de quo ante erat auditum. Sed rex 200
omnibus copiis insequebatur et VI milium passuum
intervallo a Saburra consederat. Equites missi
nocte iter conficiunt. Imprudentes atque inopinantes hostes aggrediuntur. Numidae enim quadam barbara consuetudine nullis ordinibus passim 205
consederant. Hos oppressos somno et dispersos
adorti magnum eorum numerum interficiunt ; multi
perterriti profugiunt. Quo facto ad Curionem
equites revertuntur captivosque ad eum reducunt.

Elated by this success Curio rashly presses on.

39. Curio cum omnibus copiis quarta vigilia 210
exierat, cohortibus V castris praesidio relictis.
Progressus milia passuum VI equites convenit,
rem gestam cognovit, e captivis quaerit quis castris
ad Bagradam praesit. Respondent Saburram. Reliqua studio itineris conficiendi quaerere praeter- 215
mittit, proximaque respiciens signa, ' Videtisne ',
inquit, ' milites, captivorum orationem cum perfugis
convenire. Abesse regem, exiguas esse copias

missas, quae paucis equitibus pares non esse
220 potuerint. Proinde ad praedam, ad gloriam pro-
perate ut iam de praemiis vestris et de referenda
gratia cogitare incipiamus.' Erant per se magna
quae gesserant equites, praesertim cum eorum
exiguus numerus cum tanta multitudine Numi-
225 darum conferretur. Haec tamen ab ipsis inflatius
commemorabantur, ut de suis homines laudibus
libenter praedicant. Multa praeterea spolia prae-
ferebantur. Capti homines equitesque produce-
bantur, ut quidquid intercedebat temporis, hoc
230 omne victoriam morari videretur. Ita spei Curionis
militum studia non deerant. Equites iubet sequi
sese, iterque accelerat, ut quam maxime ex fuga
perterritos adoriri posset. At illi itinere totius
noctis confecti subsequi non poterant, atque alii alio
235 loco resistebant. Ne haec quidem res Curionem
ad spem morabatur.

*Juba and his lieutenant Saburra set their trap for
Curio, and he marches into it.*

40. Iuba, certior factus a Saburra de nocturno
proelio, II milia Hispanorum et Gallorum equitum
quos suae custodiae causa circum se habere con-
240 suerat, et peditum eam partem cui maxime confid-
ebat Saburrae summisit; ipse cum reliquis copiis
elephantisque LX lentius subsequitur. Suspicatus

praemissis equitibus ipsum adfore Curionem, Saburra
copias equitum peditumque instruit, atque his
imperat ut simulatione timoris paulatim cedant 245
ac pedem referant : sese cum opus esset signum
proelii daturum, et quod rem postulare cognovisset
imperaturum. Curio, ad superiorem spem addita
praesentis temporis opinione, hostes fugere arbitratus copias ex locis superioribus in campum ducit. 250
Quibus ex locis cum longius esset progressus,
confecto iam labore exercitu xvi milium spatio
constitit. Dat signum suis Saburra, aciem constituit et circumire ordines atque hortari incipit.
Sed peditatu dumtaxat procul ad speciem utitur, 255
equites in aciem mittit.

*Battle is joined, and the enemy's tactics prove successful.
Curio's army loses heart.*

41. Non deest negotio Curio, suosque hortatur
ut spem omnem in virtute reponant. Ne militibus
quidem, ut defessis, neque equitibus, ut paucis et
labore confectis, studium ad pugnandum virtusque 260
deerat ; sed hi erant numero cc, reliqui in itinere
substiterant. Hi, quamcumque in partem impetum
fecerant, hostes loco cedere cogebant, sed neque
longius fugientes prosequi nec vehementius equos
incitare poterant. At equitatus hostium ab utroque 265
cornu circuire aciem nostram et aversos proterere in-

cipit. Cum cohortes ex acie procucurrissent, Numidae integri celeritate impetum nostrorum effugiebant, rursusque ad ordines suos se recipientes circuibant 270 et ab acie excludebant. Sic neque in loco manere ordinesque servare, neque procurrere et casum subire tutum videbatur. Hostium copiae summissis ab rege auxiliis crebro augebantur ; nostros vires lassitudine deficiebant. Simul ei qui vulnera 275 acceperant neque acie excedere neque in locum tutum referri poterant, quod tota acies equitatu hostium circumdata tenebatur. Hi de sua salute desperantes, ut extremo vitae tempore homines facere consuerunt, aut suam mortem miserabantur 280 aut parentes suos commendabant, si quos ex eo periculo fortuna servare potuisset. Plena erant omnia timoris et luctus.

An attempt to retreat is frustrated. Curio refuses to leave his men and is slain fighting.

42. Curio, ubi perterritis omnibus neque cohortationes suas neque preces audiri intelligit, unam, ut 285 in miseris rebus, spem reliquam salutis esse arbitratus, proximos colles capere universos atque eo signa inferri iubet. Hos quoque praeoccupat missus a Saburra equitatus. Tum vero ad summam desperationem nostri perveniunt, et partim fugientes 290 ab equitatu interficiuntur, partim integri procum-

bunt. Hortatur Curionem Cn. Domitius, praefectus equitum cum paucis equitibus circumsistens ut fuga salutem petat atque in castra contendat, et se ab eo non discessurum pollicetur. At Curio numquam se amisso exercitu, quem a Caesare fidei 295 suae commissum acceperit, in eius conspectum reversurum confirmat, atque ita proelians interficitur. Equites perpauci ex proelio se recipiunt. Sed ei quos equorum reficiendorum causa substitisse demonstratum est, fuga totius exercitus procul 300 animadversa, sese incolumes in castra conferunt. Milites ad unum omnes interficiuntur.

The fleet and the merchantmen leave the defeated army to its fate.

43. His rebus cognitis, M. Rufus quaestor in castris relictus a Curione cohortatur suos ne animo deficiant. Illi orant atque obsecrant ut in Siciliam 305 navibus reportentur. Pollicetur magistrisque imperat navium ut primo vespere omnes scaphas ad litus appulsas habeant. Sed tantus fuit omnium terror ut alii adesse copias Iubae dicerent, alii cum legionibus instare Varum, iamque se pulverem venientium 310 cernere (quarum rerum nihil omnino acciderat), alii classem hostium celeriter advolaturam suspicarentur. Itaque perterritis omnibus sibi quisque consulebat. Qui in classe erant proficisci impera-

315 bant. Horum fuga navium onerariarum magistros
incitabat ; pauci lenunculi ad officium imperiumque
conveniebant. Sed tanta erat completis litoribus
contentio, qui potissimum ex magno numero conscenderent, ut multitudine atque onere non nulli
320 deprimerentur, reliqui hoc timore propius adire
tardarentur.

In spite of the protests of Varus, Juba orders the killing of
most of the captives, and the enslavement of the remainder.
After settling affairs at Utica, he returns to his kingdom.

44. Quibus rebus accidit ut pauci milites patresque
familiae qui aut gratia aut misericordia valerent,
aut naves adnare possent, recepti in Siciliam in-
325 columes pervenirent. Reliquae copiae, missis ad
Varum noctu legatorum numero centurionibus, sese
ei dediderunt. Quarum cohortium milites Iuba
postero die ante oppidum conspicatus, suam esse
praedicans praedam, magnam partem eorum interfici
330 iussit, paucos electos in regnum remisit, cum Varus
suam fidem ab eo laedi quereretur, neque resistere
auderet. Ipse equo in oppidum vectus, prosequentibus compluribus senatoribus, quo in numero
erant Ser. Sulpicius et Licinius Damasippus, quae
335 fieri vellet Uticae constituit atque imperavit, die-
busque post paucis se in regnum cum omnibus
copiis recepit.

(*De Bello Civili*, ii. 36-44.)

SALLUST (C. CRISPUS SALLUSTIUS)

Historian, 86–34 B.C.

The Surrender of Jugurtha to the Roman Quaestor, Sulla

In 112 B.C., a feud among the members of the reigning house in Numidia necessitated Roman interference and a declaration of war on Jugurtha. The war dragged on without a decisive engagement until Marius was elected consul in 107 B.C. The newly appointed general infused new discipline and purpose into the Roman armies, gradually reduced Jugurtha's strongholds, and, in 106 B.C., defeated the combined forces of Jugurtha and of his father-in-law Bocchus, king of Mauretania (Morocco).

The latter then deserted his son-in-law and at length was persuaded to surrender him to Sulla, Marius' quaestor.

105. Quis rebus cognitis Bocchus per litteras a Mario petivit uti Sullam ad se mitteret, cuius arbitratu communibus negotiis consuleretur. Is 340 missus cum praesidio equitum atque funditorum Balearium. Praeterea iere sagittarii et cohors Paeligna, itineris properandi causa. Sed in itinere quinto denique die Volux filius Bocchi repente in campis patentibus cum mille non amplius equitibus 345 sese ostendit, qui temere et effuse euntes Sullae aliisque omnibus et numerum ampliorem vero et

ROMAN SLINGER AND LEADEN SLING BOLTS

hostilem metum efficiebant. Igitur se quisque
expedire, arma atque tela temptare, intendere :
350 timor aliquantus, sed spes amplior, quippe victoribus
et adversum eos quos saepe vicerant. Interim
equites exploratum praemissi rem, uti erat, quietam
nuntiant.

106. Volux adveniens quaestorem appellat dicit-
355 que se a patre Boccho obviam illis, simul et praesidio
missum. Deinde eum et proximum diem sine metu
coniuncti eunt. Post, ubi castra locata et diei
vesper erat, repente Maurus incerto voltu pavens
ad Sullam adcurrit dicitque sibi ex speculatoribus
360 cognitum Iugurtham haud procul abesse, simul
uti noctu clam secum profugeret rogat atque
hortatur. Ille animo feroci negat se totiens fusum

Numidam pertimescere : virtuti suorum satis credere. Ceterum ab eodem monitus uti noctu pro-
ficisceretur, consilium adprobat ac statim milites 365
cenatos esse, in castris ignes quam creberrimos fieri,
dein prima vigilia silentio egredi iubet. Iamque
nocturno itinere fessis omnibus Sulla pariter cum
ortu solis castra metabatur, cum equites Mauri
nuntiant Iugurtham circiter duum milium intervallo 370
ante eos consedisse. Quod postquam auditum
est, tum vero ingens metus nostros invadit : credere
se proditos a Voluce et insidiis circumventos. Ac
fuere qui dicerent manu vindicandum, neque apud
illum tantum scelus inultum relinquendum. 375

107. At Sulla, quamquam eadem existimabat,
tamen ab iniuria Maurum prohibet, suos hortatur
uti fortem animum gererent : saepe antea a paucis
strenuis adversum multitudinem bene pugnatum.
Dein Volucem, quoniam hostilia faceret, Iovem 380
maximum obtestatus, ut sceleris atque perfidiae
Bocchi testis adesset, ex castris abire iubet. Ille
lacrimans orare ne ea crederet : nihil dolo factum,
ac magis calliditate Iugurthae, cui videlicet specu-
lanti iter suum cognitum esset. Ceterum, quoniam 385
neque ingentem multitudinem haberet, et spes
opesque eius ex patre suo penderent, credere illum
nihil palam ausurum, cum ipse filius testis adesset :
qua re optimum factu videri per media eius castra

390 palam transire : sese, vel praemissis vel ibidem
relictis Mauris, solum cum Sulla iturum. Ea res
uti in tali negotio probata. Ac statim profecti, quia
de improviso acciderant, dubio atque haesitante
Iugurtha incolumes transeunt. Deinde paucis die-
395 bus quo ire intenderant perventum est.

108. Ibi cum Boccho Numida quidam Aspar
nomine multum et familiariter agebat, praemissus
ab Iugurtha, postquam Sullam accitum audierat,
orator et subdole speculatum Bocchi consilia ;
400 praeterea Dabar Massugradae filius, Mauro carus
acceptusque. Quem Bocchus fidum esse Romanis
multis ante tempestatibus expertus ilico ad Sullam
nuntiatum mittit, paratum sese facere quae populus
Romanus vellet ; colloquio diem locum tempus
405 ipse deligeret, neu Iugurthae legatum pertimesceret :
consulto sese omnia cum illo integra habere, quo
res communis licentius gereretur : nam ab insidiis
eius aliter caveri nequivisse. Sed ego comperior
Bocchum magis Punica fide quam ob ea quae
410 praedicabat, simul Romanum et Numidam spe pacis
attinuisse, multumque cum animo suo volvere
solitum, Iugurtham Romanis an illi Sullam traderet :
libidinem adversum nos, metum pro nobis suasisse.

109. Igitur Sulla respondit pauca se coram Aspare
415 locuturum, cetera occulte nullo aut quam paucis-
simis praesentibus ; simul edocet quae sibi respon-

derentur. Postquam sicuti voluerat congressi, dicit
se missum a consule venisse quaesitum ab eo, pacem
an bellum agitaturus foret. Tum rex, uti praeceptum fuerat, post diem decimum redire iubet, ac 420
nihil etiam nunc decrevisse, sed illo die responsurum.
Deinde ambo in sua castra digressi. Sed ubi
plerumque noctis processit, Sulla a Boccho occulte
accersitur. Ab utroque tantummodo fidi inter-
pretes adhibentur, praeterea Dabar internuntius, 425
sanctus vir et ex sententia ambobus. Ac statim
sic rex incipit.

110. 'Numquam ego ratus sum fore uti, rex
maximus in hac terra et omnium quos novi, privato
homini gratiam deberem. Et me hercule, Sulla, 430
ante te cognitum multis orantibus, aliis ultro
egomet opem tuli, nullius indigus. Id imminutum,
quod ceteri dolere solent, ego laetor. Fuerit mihi
eguisse aliquando pretium tuae amicitiae, qua apud
meum animum nihil carius habeo. Id adeo experiri 435
licet : arma, viros, pecuniam, postremo quidquid
animo libet, sume, utere, et, quoad vives, numquam
tibi redditam gratiam putaveris : semper apud
me integra erit ; denique nihil me sciente frustra
voles. Ceterum de re publica vestra, cuius curator 440
huc missus es, paucis accipe. Bellum ego populo
Romano neque feci neque factum umquam volui,
et fines meos adversum armatos armis tutatus sum.

Id omitto, quando vobis ita placet. Gerite quod
445 vultis cum Iugurtha bellum. Ego flumen Muluccham non egrediar, neque id intrare Iugurtham
sinam. Praeterea si quid meque vobisque dignum
petiveris, haud repulsus abibis.'

111. Ad ea Sulla pro se breviter et modice, de
450 pace et communibus rebus multis disseruit. Denique regi patefecit, quod polliceretur, senatum et
populum Romanum, quoniam armis amplius
valuisset, non in gratiam habituros : faciendum
ei aliquid, quod illorum magis quam sua retulisse
455 videretur. Id adeo in promptu esse, quoniam
copiam Iugurthae haberet ; quem si Romanis
tradidisset, fore ut illi plurimum deberetur ; ami-
citiam, foedus, Numidiae partem quam nunc
peteret tum ultro adventuram. Rex primo negi-
460 tare : cognationem, adfinitatem, praeterea foedus
intervenisse. Denique saepius fatigatus lenitur
Bocchus et ex voluntate Sullae omnia se fact-
urum promittit : ceterum ad simulandam pacem,
cuius Numida defessus bello avidissimus erat,
465 quae utilia visa constituunt. Ita composito dolo
digrediuntur.

112. At rex postero die Asparem Iugurthae
legatum appellat dicitque sibi per Dabarem ex Sulla
cognitum posse condicionibus bellum poni : quam
470 ob rem regis sui sententiam exquireret. Ille laetus

(1) SILVER COIN (denarius) issued by a son of Sulla about 62 B.C., and said to represent Jugurtha.

(2) This COIN (of the same origin as (1)) depicts the actual surrender of Jugurtha. Sulla is seated on a raised chair, while before him kneels Bocchus holding an olive branch. Behind the chair kneels Jugurtha, his hands tied behind his back.

(3) SILVER COIN (denarius), 57 B.C., issued by a grandson of Sulla. The inscription reads SVLLA CO(n)S(ul).

(4) PORTRAIT OF SALLUST (in relief) on a bronze contorniate (probably used on a playing-board like draughtsmen); fourth or fifth century after Christ. The inscription reads SALVSTIVS AVTOR.

in castra Iugurthae proficiscitur. Deinde ab illo
cuncta edoctus properato itinere post diem octavum
redit ad Bocchum et ei nuntiat Iugurtham cupere
omnia quae imperarentur facere, sed Mario parum
475 confidere : saepe antea cum imperatoribus Romanis
pacem conventam frustra fuisse./ Ceterum Bocchus
si ambobus consultum et ratam pacem vellet, daret
operam ut una ab omnibus quasi de pace in colloquium veniretur, ibique sibi Sullam traderet : cum
480 talem virum in potestatem habuisset, tum fore uti
iussu senatus aut populi foedus fieret, neque hominem nobilem non sua ignavia sed ob rem publicam in
hostium potestate relictum iri.

113. Haec Maurus secum ipse diu volvens tandem
485 promisit, ceterum dolo an vere cunctatus parum
comperimus. Postea tempore et loco constituto in
colloquium uti de pace veniretur, Bocchus Sullam
modo, modo Iugurthae legatum appellare, benigne
habere, idem ambobus polliceri. Illi pariter laeti
490 ac spei bonae pleni esse. Sed nocte ea quae proxima
fuit ante diem colloquio decretum, Maurus, adhibitis amicis ac statim immutata voluntate remotis,
dicitur secum ipse multum agitavisse, vultu et
oculis pariter atque animo varius. Tamen postremo
495 Sullam accersi iubet, et ex illius sententia Numidae
insidias tendit. Deinde ubi dies advenit et ei
nuntiatum est Iugurtham haud procul abesse,

cum paucis amicis et quaestore nostro quasi obvius honoris causa procedit in tumulum facillimum visu insidiantibus. Eodem Numida cum plerisque 500 necessariis eius inermis, uti dictum erat, accedit, ac statim signo dato undique simul ex insidiis invaditur. Ceteri obtruncati : Iugurtha Sullae vinctus traditur et ab eo ad Marium deductus est.

(*De Bello Jugurthino*, chapters 105-113.)

LIVY (Titus Livius)

Historian, 59 B.C.–17 A.D.

How Horatius kept the Bridge

508 B.C., *King Porsinna of Clusium supports the royal house of the Tarquins, who have all been expelled from Rome owing to their kinship with the tyrant Superbus Tarquinius, ' Tarquin the Proud ', driven from the throne the preceding year. King Porsinna advances on the city, now a republic, and besets it closely.*

505   Cum hostes adessent, pro se quisque in urbem
ex agris demigrant, urbem ipsam saepiunt praesidiis.
Alia muris, alia Tiberi obiecto videbantur tuta.
Pons sublicius iter paene hostibus dedit, ni unus
vir fuisset, Horatius Cocles : id munimentum illo die
510 fortuna urbis Romanae habuit. Qui positus forte
in statione pontis, cum captum repentino impetu
Ianiculum atque inde citatos decurrere hostes
vidisset, trepidamque turbam suorum arma ordinesque relinquere, reprehensans singulos, obsistens
515 obtestansque, deum et hominum fidem testabatur,
nequiquam deserto praesidio eos fugere ; si transitum pontem a tergo reliquissent, iam plus hostium
in Palatio Capitolioque quam in Ianiculo fore.
Itaque monere, praedicere, ut pontem ferro, igni,

A General View of the Janiculum Hill and the Tiber

E.N.A.

520 quacumque vi possint, interrumpant : se impetum
hostium, quantum corpore uno posset obsisti,
excepturum. Vadit inde in primum aditum pontis,
insignisque inter conspecta cedentium pugna terga
obversis comminus ad ineundum proelium armis,
525 ipso miraculo audaciae obstupefecit hostes. Duos
tamen cum eo pudor tenuit, Sp. Larcium ac T.
Herminium, ambos claros genere factisque. Cum
his primam periculi procellam et quod tumultuosis-
simum pugnae erat parumper sustinuit. Deinde
530 eos quoque ipsos exigua parte pontis relicta, revocantibus qui rescindebant, cedere in tutum coegit.
Circumferens inde truces minaciter oculos ad pro-
ceres Etruscorum nunc singulos provocare, nunc
increpare omnes, servitia regum superborum, suae
535 libertatis immemores alienam oppugnatum venire.
Cunctati aliquamdiu sunt, dum alius alium, ut
proelium incipiant, circumspectant. Pudor deinde
commovit aciem, et clamore sublato undique in
unum hostem tela coniciunt. Quae cum in obiecto
540 cuncta scuto haesissent, neque ille minus obstinatus
ingenti pontem obtineret gradu, iam impetu cona-
bantur detrudere virum, cum simul fragor rupti
pontis, simul clamor Romanorum alacritate perfecti
operis sublatus, pavore subito impetum sustinuit.
545 Tum Cocles 'Tiberine pater', inquit, 'te sancte
precor, haec arma et hunc militem propitio flumine

(1)

(2)

(3)

(1), (2). ROMAN BRONZE MEDALLION, issued between A.D. 140 and 144. The reverse shows the *pons sublicius* broken down, Horatius Cocles swimming to the Roman shore, and one of the enemy hurling a missile at him. The obverse is a head of the emperor Antoninus Pius, bearing the inscription, ANTONINUS AUG(*ustus*) PIVS P(*ater*) P(*atriae*) TR(*ibunicia*) P(*otestate*) CO(*n*)S(*ul*) III.

(3) BRONZE COIN (sestertius) of the Emperor Tiberius (A.D. 14–38). See the Triumphal Procession (Frontispiece) and the note on l. 665.

accipias!' Ita sic armatus in Tiberim desiluit,
multisque superincidentibus telis incolumis ad suos
tranavit, rem ausus plus famae habituram ad
550 posteros quam fidei. Grata erga tantam virtutem
civitas fuit : statua in comitio posita, agri quantum
uno die circumaravit datum.

(Book II, chapter 10.)

The Story of Mucius Scaevola

508 B.C.

Obsidio erat nihilo minus et frumenti cum summa
caritate inopia, sedendoque expugnaturum se urbem
555 spem Porsinna habebat. Tum C. Mucius adulescens
nobilis, cui indignum videbatur populum Romanum
ab Etruscis obsideri, quorum saepe exercitus
fuderit, magno audacique aliquo facinore eam
indignitatem vindicandam ratus, primo sua sponte
560 penetrare in hostium castra constituit. Dein
metuens, ne si consulum iniussu et ignaris omnibus
iret, forte deprehensus a custodibus Romanis retraheretur ut transfuga, fortuna tum urbis crimen
adfirmante, senatum adit. ' Transire Tiberim', in-
565 quit, ' patres, et intrare, si possim, castra hostium
volo, non praedo nec populationum in vicem ultor :
maius, si di iuvant, in animo est facinus.' Ad-
probant patres.

Abdito intra vestem ferro proficiscitur. Ubi eo
venit, in confertissima turba prope regium tribunal 570
constitit. Ibi cum stipendium militibus forte dare-
tur, et scriba cum rege sedens pari fere ornatu
multa ageret, eumque milites volgo adirent, timens
sciscitari, uter Porsinna esset, ne ignorando regem
semet ipse aperiret quis esset, quo temere traxit 575
fortuna facinus, scribam pro rege obtruncat. Vadentem inde, qua per trepidam turbam cruento mucrone
sibi ipse fecerat viam, cum concursu ad clamorem
facto comprehensum regii satellites retraxissent, ante
tribunal regis destitutus, tum quoque inter tantas 580
fortunae minas metuendus magis quam metuens,
' Romanus sum', inquit ' civis, C. Mucium vocant.
Hostis hostem occidere volui, nec ad mortem minus
animi est quam fuit ad caedem : et facere et pati
fortia Romanum est. Nec unus in te ego hos animos 585
gessi ; longus post me ordo est idem petentium
decus. Proinde in hoc discrimen, si iuvat, accingere, ut in singulas horas capite dimices tuo, ferrum
hostemque in vestibulo habeas regiae. Hoc tibi
iuventus Romana indicimus bellum. Nullam aciem, 590
nullum proelium timueris ; uni tibi et cum singulis
res erit.'

Cum rex simul ira infensus periculoque conterritus
circumdari ignes minitabundus iuberet, nisi expromeret propere, quas insidiarum sibi minas per 595

ambages iaceret, 'en tibi', inquit, 'ut sentias
quam vile corpus sit eis qui magnam gloriam
vident' : dextramque accenso ad sacrificium foculo
inicit. Quam cum velut alienato ab sensu torreret
600 animo, prope attonitus miraculo rex cum ab sede
sua prosiluisset, amoverique ab altaribus iuvenem
iussisset, 'tu vero abi', inquit, 'in te magis quam
in me hostilia ausus. Iuberem macte virtute
esse, si pro mea patria ista virtus staret : nunc
605 iure belli liberum te intactum inviolatumque hinc
dimitto.'

Tunc Mucius quasi remunerans meritum, 'quando
quidem', inquit, 'est apud te virtuti honos, ut
beneficio tuleris a me quod minis nequisti : trecenti
610 coniuravimus principes iuventutis Romanae, ut
in te hac via grassaremur. Mea prima sors fuit ;
ceteri, ut cuiusque ceciderit primi, quoad te op-
portunum fortuna dederit, suo quisque tempore
aderunt.'

(Book II, chapter 12.)

The Gauls March on Rome and Plunder the City

390 B.C.   *By this date the Romans had become the dominant tribe
in Latium and had just crushed for ever their most powerful
rival, the city of Veii, in Etruria.   In this year, however,
their growing power was fated to receive a serious check.
Nomadic bands of Gauls entered Italy and, first occupying
the Lombardy Plain, began to move southwards.   They
met the Romans at the Alia and after inflicting a very
heavy defeat on them, marched on Rome three days later
and occupied the city with the exception of the Capitol.*

39. Gallos quoque velut obstupefactos miraculum 615
victoriae tam repentinae tenuit, et ipsi pavore
defixi primum steterunt, velut ignari quid acci-
disset ; deinde insidias vereri ; postremo caesorum
spolia legere armorumque cumulos, ut mos eis est,
coacervare ; tum demum, postquam nihil usquam 620
hostile cernebatur, viam ingressi haud multo ante
solis occasum ad urbem Romam perveniunt.   Ubi
cum praegressi equites non portas clausas, non
stationem pro portis excubare, non armatos esse
in muris rettulissent, aliud priori simile miraculum 625
eos sustinuit ; noctemque veriti et ignotae situm
urbis inter Romam atque Anienem consedere,
exploratoribus missis circa moenia aliasque portas,
quaenam hostibus in perdita re consilia essent.
Romani cum, quoniam pars maior ex acie Veios 630
petisset quam Romam, neminem superesse praeter
eos qui Romam refugerant, crederent, complorati

omnes pariter vivi mortuique totam prope urbem
lamentis impleverunt. Privatos deinde luctus stupe-
635 fecit publicus pavor, postquam hostes adesse
nuntiatum est ; mox ululatus cantusque dissonos
vagantibus circa moenia turmatim barbaris audie-
bant. Omne inde tempus suspensos ita tenuit
animos usque ad lucem alteram, ut identidem iam
640 in urbem futurus videretur impetus : primo adventu, quia accesserant ad urbem : mansuros
enim ad Aliam fuisse, nisi hoc consilium foret ;
deinde sub occasum solis, quia haud multum diei
supererat ; tum in noctem dilatum consilium esse,
645 quo plus pavoris inferrent ; postremo lux ad-
propinquans exanimare ; timorique perpetuo ipsum
malum continens fuit, cum signa infesta portis
sunt inlata.

Nequaquam tamen ea nocte neque insequenti
650 die similis illi, quae ad Aliam tam pavide fugerat,
civitas fuit. Nam cum defendi urbem posse tam
parva relicta manu spes nulla esset, placuit cum
coniugibus ac liberis iuventutem militarem sena-
tusque robur in arcem Capitoliumque concedere,
655 armisque et frumento collato inde ex loco munito
deos hominesque et Romanum nomen defendere ;
flaminem sacerdotesque vestales sacra publica a
caede, ab incendiis procul auferre, nec ante deseri
cultum deorum, quam non superessent qui colerent.

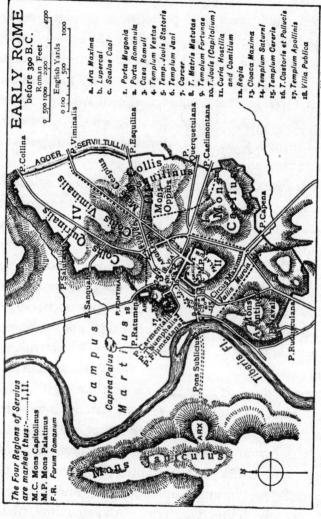

EARLY ROME
before 390 B.C.

Roman Feet
500 1000   2000   4000

English Yards
0 100   500   1000

a. Ara Maxima
b. Lupercal
c. Scalae Caci

1. Porta Mugonia
2. Porta Romanula
3. Casa Romuli
4. Templum Vestae
5. Temp. Jovis Statoris
6. Templum Jani
7. Carcer
8. T. Matris Matutae
9. Templum Fortunae
10. T. Jovis (Capitolium)
11. Curia Hostilia and Comitium
12. Regia
13. Cloaca Maxima
14. Templum Saturni
15. Templum Cereris
16. T. Castoris et Pollucis
17. Templum Apollinis
18. Villa Publica

The Four Regions of Servius are marked thus:— I, II.
M.C. Mons Capitolinus
M.P. Mons Palatinus
F.R. Forum Romanum

Walker & Cockerell sc.

660 Si arx Capitoliumque, sedes deorum, si senatus, caput publici consilii, si militaris iuventus superfuerit imminenti ruinae urbis, facilem iacturam esse seniorum relictae in urbe utique periturae turbae. Et quo id aequiore animo de plebe multi-
665 tudo ferret, senes triumphales consularesque simul se cum illis palam dicere obituros, nec his corporibus, quibus non arma ferre, non tueri patriam possent, oneraturos inopiam armatorum.

40. Haec inter seniores morti destinatos iactata
670 solacia. Versae inde adhortationes ad agmen iuvenum quos in Capitolium atque in arcem prosequebantur, commendantes virtuti eorum iuventaeque urbis per trecentos sexaginta annos omnibus bellis victricis quaecumque reliqua esset fortuna. Di-
675 gredientibus qui spem omnem atque opem secum ferebant, ab eis qui captae urbis non superesse statuerant exitio, cum ipsa res speciesque miserabilis erat, tum muliebris fletus et concursatio incerta nunc hos nunc illos sequentium rogitantium-
680 que viros natosque, cui se fato darent, nihil quod humani superesset mali, relinquebant. Magna pars tamen earum in arcem suos persecutae sunt nec prohibente ullo nec vocante, quia, quod utile obsessis ad minuendam imbellem multitudinem,
685 id parum humanum erat. Alia maxime plebis turba, quam nec capere tam exiguus collis nec

ROME'S NEIGHBOURS.

Roman Miles
0 5 10 20 30 40 50

English Miles
0 5 10 20 30 40 50

Walker & Cockerell sc.

alere in tanta inopia frumenti poterat, ex urbe
effusa velut agmine iam uno petiit Ianiculum.
Inde pars per agros dilapsi, pars urbes petunt
690 finitimas, sine ullo duce aut consensu, suam quisque
spem, sua consilia communibus deploratis sequentes.

41. Romae interim, satis iam omnibus ut in tali
re ad tuendam arcem compositis, turba seniorum
domos regressi adventum hostium obstinato ad
695 mortem animo exspectabant. Qui eorum curules
gesserant magistratus, ut in fortunae pristinae
honorumque ac virtutis insignibus morerentur,
quae augustissima vestis est tensas ducentibus
triumphantibusve, ea vestiti medio aedium eburneis
700 sellis sedere.

Galli ingressi postero die urbem patente Collina
porta in forum perveniunt, circumferentes oculos
ad templa deum arcemque solam belli speciem
tenentem. Inde modico relicto praesidio, ne quis
705 in dissipatos ex arce aut Capitolio impetus fieret,
dilapsi ad praedam vacuis occursu hominum viis,
pars in proxima quaeque tectorum agmine ruunt,
pars ultima, velut ea demum intacta et referta
praeda, petunt. Inde rursus ipsa solitudine ab-
710 sterriti, ne qua fraus hostilis vagos exciperet, in
forum ac propinqua foro loca conglobati redibant.

Ubi haud secus quam venerabundi intuebantur
in aedium vestibulis sedentes viros, praeter orna-

tum habitumque humano augustiorem maiestate
etiam, simillimos dis. Ad eos velut ad simulacra 715
versi cum starent, M. Papirius, unus ex eis, dicitur
Gallo barbam suam permulcenti scipione eburneo
in caput incusso iram movisse, atque ab eo initium
caedis ortum, ceteros in sedibus suis trucidatos ;
post principum caedem nulli deinde mortalium parci, 720
diripi tecta, exhaustis inici ignes.

(Book V, chapters 39-41.)

CICERO (Marcus Tullius Cicero)

Statesman, Orator, and Man of Letters (106–43 B.C.)

Murder on the Appian Way

(An extract from Cicero's speech Pro Milone, ' In Defence of Milo ')

At the trial of Milo, accused of having murdered Clodius on January 18th, 52 B.C., Cicero relates the incidents which led up to the meeting of the two rivals, Clodius and Milo, and the scuffle in which Clodius was fatally injured.

Cicero admits the charge, but pleads justifiable homicide. The whole of the following narrative aims at proving, first, that Clodius desired to kill Milo, as the only obstacle to his own lawless activities, and secondly, that it was Clodius who ambushed Milo, not Milo Clodius.

24. P. Clodius, cum statuisset omni scelere in praetura vexare rem publicam videretque ita tracta esse comitia anno superiore ut non multos menses
725 praeturam gerere posset, qui non honoris gradum spectaret, ut ceteri, sed et L. Paulum collegam effugere vellet, singulari virtute civem, et annum integrum ad dilacerandam rem publicam quaereret, subito reliquit annum suum seseque in proximum
730 transtulit, non, ut fit, religione aliqua, sed ut haberet, quod ipse dicebat, ad praeturam gerendam,

hoc est ad evertendam rem publicam, plenum annum atque integrum.

25. Occurrebat ei mancam ac debilem praeturam futuram suam consule Milone : eum porro summo 735 consensu populi Romani consulem fieri videbat. Contulit se ad eius competitores, sed ita totam ut petitionem ipse solus etiam invitis illis gubernaret, tota ut comitia suis, ut dictitabat, umeris sustineret. Convocabat tribus, se interponebat. Quanto ille 740 plura miscebat, tanto hic magis in dies convalescebat. Ubi vidit homo ad omne facinus paratissimus fortissimum virum, inimicissimum suum, certissimum consulem, idque intellexit non solum sermonibus, sed etiam suffragiis populi Romani saepe 745 esse declaratum, palam agere coepit et aperte dicere occidendum Milonem.

26. Servos agrestes et barbaros, quibus silvas publicas depopulatus erat Etruriamque vexarat, ex Appennino deduxerat, quos videbatis. Res erat 750 minime obscura. Etenim dictitabat palam consulatum Miloni eripi non posse, vitam posse. Significavit hoc saepe in senatu, dixit in contione ; quin etiam M. Favonio, fortissimo viro, quaerenti ex eo qua spe fureret Milone vivo, respondit triduo illum 755 aut summum quadriduo esse periturum ; quam vocem eius ad hunc M. Catonem statim Favonius detulit.

27. Interim cum sciret Clodius—neque enim erat
760 id difficile scire a Lanuvinis—iter sollemne, legiti-
mum, necessarium ante diem XIII Kalendas Feb-
ruarias Miloni esse Lanuvium ad flaminem prodendum, quod erat dictator Lanuvi Milo, Roma
subito ipse profectus pridie est ut ante suum
765 fundum, quod re intellectum est, Miloni insidias
collocaret ; atque ita profectus est ut contionem
turbulentam in qua eius furor desideratus est, quae
illo ipso die habita est, relinqueret, quam, nisi obire
facinoris locum tempusque voluisset, numquam
770 reliquisset.

28. Milo autem cum in senatu fuisset eo die quoad
senatus est dimissus, domum venit, calceos et
vestimenta mutavit, paulisper, dum se uxor, ut
fit, comparat, commoratus est, dein profectus id
775 temporis cum iam Clodius, si quidem eo die Romam
venturus erat, redire potuisset. Obviam fit ei
Clodius, expeditus, in equo, nulla raeda, nullis
impedimentis, nullis Graecis comitibus, ut solebat,
sine uxore, quod numquam fere : cum hic insidiator,
780 qui iter illud ad caedem faciendam apparasset, cum
uxore veheretur in raeda, paenulatus, magno et
impedito ancillarum puerorumque comitatu.

29. Fit obviam Clodio ante fundum eius hora
fere undecima aut non multo secus. Statim com-
785 plures cum telis in hunc faciunt de loco superiore

THE APPIAN WAY A FEW MILES SOUTH OF ROME
In the distance are the Alban Hills.

E.N.

impetum ; adversi raedarium occidunt. Cum autem
hic de raeda reiecta paenula desiluisset seque
acri animo defenderet, illi qui erant cum Clodio
gladiis eductis, partim recurrere ad raedam ut a
790 tergo Milonem adorirentur, partim, quod hunc
iam interfectum putarent, caedere incipiunt eius
servos qui post erant ; ex quibus qui animo fideli
in dominum et praesenti fuerunt, partim occisi
sunt, partim, cum ad raedam pugnari viderent,
795 domino succurrere prohiberentur, Milonem occisum
et ex ipso Clodio audirent et re vera putarent,
fecerunt id servi Milonis—dicam enim aperte non
derivandi criminis causa, sed ut factum est—nec
imperante nec sciente nec praesente domino, quod
800 suos quisque servos in tali re facere voluisset.

30. Haec sicuti exposui ita gesta sunt, iudices :
insidiator superatus est, vi victa vis vel potius
oppressa virtute audacia est. Nihil dico quid res
publica consecuta sit, nihil quid vos, nihil quid
805 omnes boni : nihil sane id prosit Miloni, qui hoc
fato natus est ut ne se quidem servare potuerit
quin una rem publicam vosque servaret. Si id
iure fieri non potuit, nihil habeo quod defendam.
Sin hoc et ratio doctis et necessitas barbaris et
810 mos gentibus et feris natura ipsa praescripsit ut
omnem semper vim quacumque ope possent a
corpore, a capite, a vita sua propulsarent, non

potestis hoc facinus improbum iudicare quin simul
iudicetis omnibus qui in latrones inciderint aut
illorum telis aut vestris sententiis esse pereundum. 815

(*Pro Milone*, Sections 24-30.)

A Letter to Atticus

*In this letter to his great friend Atticus, Cicero informs him of
the latest political news (i.e. the complaints of Pompey and
the complete unanimity of the senatorial party) and
expresses his fears [1] of Clodius' activities and probable
election to the tribunate. He concludes with an urgent
appeal to his friend to come to Rome.*

Summer or Autumn 59 B.C.

Numquam ante arbitror te epistulam meam
legisse nisi mea manu scriptam. Ex eo colligere
poteris, quanta occupatione distinear. Nam cum
vacui temporis nihil haberem et cum recreandae
voculae causa necesse esset mihi ambulare, haec 820
dictavi ambulans.

Primum igitur illud te scire volo, Sampsiceramum,
nostrum amicum, vehementer sui status paenitere,
restituique in eum locum cupere, ex quo decidit,
doloremque suum impertire nobis et medicinam 825
interdum aperte quaerere, quam ego posse inveniri
nullam puto ; deinde omnes illius partis auctores

[1] These fears were well-grounded. One of Clodius' first
acts as tribune in 58 B.C. was to secure the expulsion of
Cicero from Italy. See the note on Pro Milone, l. 722.

GNAEUS POMPEIUS MAGNUS (SAMPSICERAMUS)

ac socios nullo adversario consenescere, consensionem
universorum nec voluntatis nec sermonis maiorem
umquam fuisse. 830

Nos autem—nam id te scire cupere certo scio—
publicis consiliis nullis intersumus totosque nos ad
forensem operam laboremque contulimus. Ex quo,
quod facile intellegi possit, in multa commemoratione
earum rerum quas gessimus desiderioque versamur. 835
Sed βοώπιδος nostrae consanguineus non mediocres
terrores iacit atque denuntiat, et Sampsiceramo
negat, ceteris prae se fert et ostentat. Quam ob
rem, si me amas tantum quantum profecto amas,
si dormis, expergiscere, si stas, ingredere, si vero 840
ingrederis, curre, si curris, advola. Credibile non
est quantum ego in consiliis, prudentia tua, quod
maximum est, quantum in amore et fide ponam.
Magnitudo rei longam orationem fortasse desiderat,
coniunctio vero nostrorum animorum brevitate 845
contenta est. Permagni nostra interest te, si
comitiis non potueris, at declarato illo esse Romae.
Cura ut valeas.

(*Letters to Atticus*, ii. 23.)

The Friendship of Laelius and Scipio

In this extract from Cicero's essay ' On Friendship ', [1] *Laelius tells his friends of the loss of his great friend, Scipio the Younger, and of the consolation he finds in the fact that no harm has happened to him and that he died after a most brilliant career when he had received every mark of honour from his grateful country.*

Ego si Scipionis desiderio me moveri negem,
850 quam id recte faciam viderint sapientes ; sed certe
mentiar. Moveor enim tali amico orbatus, qualis,
ut arbitror, nemo unquam erit, ut confirmare
possum, nemo certe fuit. Sed non egeo medicina ;
me ipse consolor et maxime illo solacio, quod eo
855 errore careo quo amicorum decessu plerique angi
solent. Nihil mali accidisse Scipioni puto ; mihi
accidit si quid accidit. Suis autem incommodis
graviter angi non amicum, sed se ipsum amantis est.
Cum illo vero quis neget actum esse praeclare?
860 Nisi enim, quod ille minime putabat, immortali-
tatem optare vellet, quid non est adeptus quod
homini fas esset optare? qui summam spem civium,
quam de eo iam puero habuerant, continuo adulescens incredibili virtute superavit ; qui consulatum
865 petivit nunquam, factus est consul bis ; primum
ante tempus, iterum sibi suo tempore, rei publicae
paene sero ; qui duabus urbibus eversis inimicis-

[1] Written in 44 B.C.

simis huic imperio non modo praesentia, verum
etiam futura bella delevit. Quid dicam de moribus
facillimis, de pietate in matrem, liberalitate in 870
sorores, bonitate in suos, iustitia in omnes? Nota
sunt vobis. Quam autem civitati carus fuerit,
maerore funeris indicatum est. Quid igitur hunc
paucorum annorum accessio iuvare potuisset?
Senectus enim quamvis non sit gravis, ut memini 875
Catonem anno ante quam mortuus est, mecum et
cum Scipione disserere, tamen aufert eam viriditatem in qua etiamnunc erat Scipio.

Quam ob rem vita quidem talis fuit vel fortuna
vel gloria ut nihil posset accedere : moriendi autem 880
sensum celeritas abstulit. Quo de genere mortis
difficile dictu est ; quid homines suspicentur videtis.
Hoc vere tamen licet dicere, P. Scipioni ex multis
diebus quos in vita celeberrimos laetissimosque
viderit, illum diem clarissimum fuisse, cum Senatu 885
dimisso domum reductus ad vesperum est a patribus
conscriptis, populo Romano, sociis et Latinis,
pridie quam excessit e vita, ut ex tam alto dignitatis
gradu ad superos videatur deos potius quam ad
inferos pervenisse.

890

(*De Amicitia*, chapter iii.)

NOTES

*The Rise and Fall of Miltiades, the Athenian
General and Statesman*

CHAPTER 3

Line 1. **Eisdem temporibus,** about 515 B.C.

l. 2. **Scythis.** The Scythians were a nomad people, who inhabited the parts of Europe between the Carpathian mountains and the R. Don. They were expert horsemen.

l. 3. **in Histro flumine,** the lower part of the Danube.

l. 4. **qua . . . traduceret.** Note the subjunctive mood which expresses purpose, ' whereby to lead '. **Qua = quā viā.**

l. 4. **dum ipse abesset.** The subjunctive mood shows that this sentence is part of Darius' thought (virtual indirect speech).

l. 5. **custodes,** in apposition with **principes,** ' as guardians '.

l. 5. **ex Ionia et Aeolide.** Ionia was the name given to the west coast of Asia Minor which had been colonised from 900 B.C. onwards by Greek-speaking peoples from the mainland. Aeolis was the name given to the northern strip by the Hellespont. All the Greek inhabitants of this seaboard had been incorporated by Darius into the Persian Empire.

l. 7. **facillime putavit . . . potestate.** Order for translation : putavit se facillime retenturum (esse) sub sua potestate loquentes (those speaking) Graeca lingua (abl.) qui incolerent Asiam.

l. 8. **Asiam,** i.e. Asia Minor.

l. 10. oppida tuenda, ' towns to be guarded '.

l. 10. se oppresso, ablative absolute, ' himself (having been) crushed '. Translate by a conditional clause, ' if he were crushed '.

l. 12. cui . . . crederetur, ' (as one) to whom the charge (of the bridge) might be entrusted '. For the subjunctive, see the note on l. 4. At this time, the Athenian hero was governor or tyrant of the Chersonese (Peninsula of Gallipoli), which had been seized for the Athenians by Miltiades' uncle. When Athens became a strong imperial and commercial power in the fifth century B.C., the Chersonese possessed enormous strategic importance, situated as it was on the great trade-route (corn and wool) from South Russia to Greece.

l. 12. hic, ' hereupon '.

l. 13. male rem . . . a Scythis. By retreating and adopting a ' scorched earth ' policy, the Scythians led the unwieldy forces of Darius on a wild-goose chase over the barren steppes of Russia. This failure to win a decisive action, coupled with a lack of supplies, compelled the Persian king to withdraw and thus suffer a considerable loss of prestige which led the subject Greek cities of Asia Minor eventually to revolt against his rule.

l. 15. liberandae Graeciae, ' of Greece to be freed ', i.e. ' of freeing Greece '. Note the gerundive construction, which in the genitive is an alternative to the gerund with a direct object, **liberandi Graeciam.**

ll. 16-22. nam . . . interiturum, indirect speech, dependent on, ' he said ', which can easily be supplied from **hortatus est.** Note that the verbs in the subordinate clauses are in the subjunctive *except* **transportarat.** This indicative shows that the relative clause is an addition by Nepos and not part of Miltiades' argument or speech.

l. 17. transportarat = transportaverat. In verb forms containing the letter ' v ', this and the following vowel often disappear.

l. 19. **Graeci genere,** ' Greeks by birth ', is in apposition with the subject of incolerent.

l. 21. **ponte rescisso.** Translate by a conditional clause. See the note on l. 10 above.

l. 23. **Histiaeus ... obstitit,** ' Histiaeus of Miletus hindered that the thing should not be accomplished ', i.e. ' prevented his purpose from being effected '.

l. 24. **non idem ... multitudini,** ' that the same thing was not expedient for themselves who held the supreme power as (*lit.*, and) for the people '. Idem is neuter.

l. 27. **quo exstincto.** See the note on l. 10 above.

l. 27. **ipsos** = se ipsos. Similarly in l. 29, ipsis = sibi ipsis.

l. 27. **civibus ... daturos** (esse), ' would pay retribution to their fellow-citizens ' = ' would be punished by their fellow-citizens '. Poenas do is regularly used as the passive of punio (4), ' I punish '.

l. 31. **tam multis consciis,** ablative absolute, ' so many (being) privy (to them) ', = ' while *or* since so many were privy to them '. Note that the ablative absolute may be translated in a variety of ways. So far, we have had these phrases rendered by conditional and causal clauses.

l. 34. **cuius ratio,** ' his plan '. For cuius, see the note on Caesar, Chap. 36, l. 167.

l. 35. **est laudanda,** ' is to be praised ', *or* ' should be praised '. In the nominative, the gerundive expresses ' ought ', ' must ', ' should '.

l. 35. **cum,** ' since '.

CHAPTER 4

Line 37. **autem,** ' now '. It is often thus used in narrative where a transition is made.

l. 38. **hortantibus amicis.** Translate the ablative absolute by a causal (' since ') clause. ' Since his friends encouraged him ', etc.

l. 41. **ducenta.** Supply milia from the following milia.

l. 42. **causam interserens**, ' alleging (as) a reason '.

l. 42. **quod . . . expugnassent . . . interfecissent**. Note the subjunctive mood, due to the causal clause being subordinate in indirect speech and representing the thought of Darius.

l. 43. **eorum auxilio**. When the Ionian Greeks of the coastal towns of Asia Minor revolted in 501 B.C. against the rule of Darius, they appealed to the mainland Greeks to send assistance. Only Athens and Eretria (in Euboea) answered the call, the former sending twenty, the latter five ships. The rebels successfully stormed Sardis, the residenc of the Persian governor.

l. 45. **classe . . . appulsa**. Translate this ablative absolute by a participial phrase, ' having put in their fleet '.

l. 45. **ad Euboeam**, ' at Euboea '.

l. 46. **cives abreptos . . . miserunt**, ' they sent into Asia the citizens (having been) carried off ', i.e. ' they carried off the citizens and sent them into Asia '.

For this translation, cf. **nuntium captum interfecerunt**, ' they killed the captured messenger ', i.e. ' they captured and killed the messenger '.

l. 54. **hemerodromoe**, *lit.*, ' day-runners ', i.e. ' couriers who can run all day '. Herodotus, the Greek historian, says that Philippides, whom he calls Phidippides, ran the distance between Athens and Sparta, the capital of the Lacedaemonians (140 miles) in 48 hours.

l. 54. **quam . . . esset auxilio**, ' how quickly they wanted assistance ', *lit.*, ' how quick help there was need of '. **opus**, ' need ', ' want ', is used with *a dative of the person who wants and the ablative of the thing wanted* ', e.g. **opus est mihi equo**, ' I want a horse '.

l. 55. **praetores**, ' generals '.

l. 56. **qui . . . praeessent**. The subjunctive expresses purpose.

l. 57. **utrum . . . defenderent . . . irent . . . decernerent**, ' whether they should defend . . . or go . . . and fight it

out '. Note these good examples of the indirect deliberative subjunctive.

In direct speech, the generals would have said, **defen-
damus,** ' are we to defend ', etc.

l. 59. **unus,** ' only '.

l. 60. **primo quoque tempore,** ' at the very first opportunity ' ; **quoque** is the ablative of **quisque.**

ll. 60-63. **id . . . tardiores,** indirect speech, ' if this was
done, courage would be added to the citizens . . . and the
enemy would be delayed for the same reason . . .'.

Note **accessurum,** the future infinitive of **accedere,** which
is often used as the passive of **addo,** ' I add '.

l. 61. **cum . . . desperari.** **desperari** is the present infinitive passive, which in direct speech would be **despera-
tur,** ' men despair '. Note the *impersonal* use of intransitive
verbs in the passive, and cf. **pugnatur,** ' fighting is being
done ' =' men fight ', ' they fight '.

l. 63. **auderi.** See the preceding note.

CHAPTER 5

Line 65. Atheniensibus auxilio, *lit.,* ' for a help to the
Athenians '. Note **auxilio,** dative of purpose, with **Atheniensibus,** dative of advantage.

l. 66. **praeter Plataeenses.** Plataea was a small town
about forty miles north-west of Athens.

l. 69. **quo factum est ut,** ' by which it happened that ' =
' thus it happened that '.

l. 73. **sub montis . . . apertissima.** Order for translation :
acie instructa sub montis radicibus regione non apertissima.

l. 75. **namque arbores . . . rarae.** The Persian cavalry
was by far the greatest menace to the Athenians. Thus
the latter encamped on the foothills of Mt. Pentelicus and
avoided the level places where the Persian cavalry would
have freedom of movement. Moreover, they placed tree-

trunks at intervals (*rarae*), further to protect their flank. Cf. the modern use of tank-traps.

l. 75. hoc consilio ut, ' with this purpose that '.

l. 77. equitatus, nominative.

l. 77. ne . . . clauderentur, ' lest they (i.e. the Athenians) might be hemmed in by superior numbers '.

l. 80. eoque magis quod . . ., ' and the more so, because . . .'.

l. 81. priusquam . . . venirent, ' before the Lacedaemonians could come for a support ', i.e. ' to support them '.

Note that the subjunctive mood is used in temporal clauses, when some other idea besides that of time is added. Here for example there is a suggestion of anticipation.

subsidio, dative of purpose.

l. 84. in quo . . . Athenienses, ' in this (battle) the A. were (by) so much superior in valour '.

Note tanto, ablative of the measure of difference, found chiefly with comparatives.

l. 86. profligarint. See the note on l. 17.

l. 87. qua pugna . . . nobilius, ' up to this time nothing has been more famous than this battle '. Note qua pugna, ablative of comparison.

Chapter 6

Line 90. Cuius victoriae . . . docere. Order for translation : non videtur alienum (out of place) docere quale praemium cuius (=this) victoriae sit tributum Miltiadi.

l. 91. quo facilius . . . possit. Note that in a purpose clause containing a comparative, ut is replaced by quo.

l. 94. rari et tenues, ' infrequent and rare '. These two adjectives are to be contrasted with effusi, ' unreserved ' and obsoleti, ' common ', in l. 95.

l. 97. liberarat =liberaverat. See the note on l. 17.

l. 98. talis honos . . . poneretur. Order for translation : talis honos tributus est (huic Miltiadi) ut cum pugna Marathonia depingeretur in porticu quae vocatur Poecile, eius imago poneretur prima in numero decem praetorum.

l. 98. **Poecile.** The ' Painted ' or ' Decorated ' Porch at Athens contained paintings of famous battles. We learn that the battle of Marathon in which Miltiades was shown exhorting and leading his men into battle was painted by order of Miltiades' son, Cimon.

l. 104. **Demetrio Phalereo ;** Demetrius of Phalerus [1] was governor of Athens in 317 B.C., when the once famous city, the home of democracy, had become subject to the Macedonian kings.

CHAPTER 7

Line 107. **insulas,** i.e. islands in the Aegean Sea. In their expedition Datis and Artaphernes sailed across the Aegean Sea via Naxos and other islands. No doubt these islands had been compelled to furnish supplies and water to the Persian fleet.

l. 109. **quo imperio,** ' by means of this command '.

l. 111. **cum,** ' since '.

l. 112. **operibus,** ' with siege works '.

l. 113. **vineis ac testudinibus constitutis,** ' having erected mantlets and pent-houses '. In Roman times both **vineae** and **testudines** were covered galleries, made of wood and wicker-work and protected against fire by raw hides. They were pushed up against the enemy's wall, and under their protection the besiegers tried to undermine and breach it.

l. 114. **cum . . . potiretur,** ' when it was at that point (**in eo**) that he was obtaining possession of the town ' = ' when he was on the point of obtaining . . .'. Note that **potior** (4) is followed by the ablative case.

l. 115. **in continenti,** ' on the mainland ', should refer to Asia Minor, but it is too far away to be seen from Paros.

l. 116. **nescio quo casu,** ' I know not by what chance ', = ' by some chance or other '.

---

[1] Phalerus was a district in Attica.

l. 118. **ut**, ' when '. Note that in this meaning **ut is** followed by the *indicative* mood.

l. 119. **utrisque venit in opinionem**, ' it came into the belief to both sides ', = ' both sides came to believe '. Note that in the plural, **uterque**, ' each (of two) ', means ' each of two sides or parties '.

l. 120. **quo factum est ut.** See the note on l. 69 above.

l. 122. **incensis operibus**, ' the siege-works having been burned '. Render by a participial phrase, ' burning the siege-works '.

l. 122. **cum totidem navibus atque,** ' with as many ships as '.

l. 124. **magna cum offensione civium suorum**, ' to the great disgust of his fellow-citizens '. **civium is a** good example of a subjective genitive.

l. 126. **infectis rebus**, ' things not-done ', ablative absolute, = ' without success '.

l. 129. **quoniam . . . posset.** quoniam is followed by the *indicative* mood unless it is found in Indirect Speech (*Oratio Obliqua*), either Partial or Complete. So here, we may explain the mood, by regarding the causal clause as an indirect quotation from the speech of Miltiades' brother Stesagoras.

l. 130. **causa cognita**, ' when the case was examined '.

l. 130. **eapitis absolutus**, ' acquitted on a capital charge '. **capitis** depends on **crimine**, ' charge ', understood.

l. 131. **pecunia multatus est**, ' he was fined '; *lit.*, ' he was punished in money '.

According to Athenian law, after speeches had been made on both sides, the accuser proposed one penalty, and the accused another, while the task of the jury was to decide between the two penalties thus put before them. In this particular trial, Miltiades' accusers proposed the penalty of death, and his friends proposed a fine of 50 talents. The jury chose the latter. It is important for us to remember that the jury had no option but to choose one of the two penalties proposed. For example, at the famous trial of the celebrated Socrates in 399 B.C., his accusers proposed the death sentence and Socrates, after playfully suggesting that he ought to receive free meals and lodging as a benefactor to his country, then proposed a trifling fine. The result was that by a small majority, the jurymen chose the death penalty.

l. 132. quantus . . erat, ' (as much) as the expense that had been laid out on the fleet '.

l. 134. in vincula publica, i.e. ' into prison '.

l. 135. diem obiit supremum, ' he met his last day ', i.e. ' he died '.

Chapter 8

Line 136. crimine Pario, ' on the charge concerning Paros '.

l. 138. Pisistrati. Pisistratus was tyrant of Athens from 550-527 B.C., and his sons, Hipparchus and Hippias, maintained a similar government until the former was slain in 514 B.C., and the latter was compelled to resign in 510 B.C. Actually, the government of Pisistratus was not tyrannical, for he maintained many of the democratic institutions of Athens, while, of his sons, Hippias alone showed signs of tyrannical behaviour, and then only after the murder of his brother. As far as we can judge, the assassination of Hipparchus was the result of a lover's quarrel and had no political significance.

The date of Miltiades' trial is 489 B.C.

l. 140. Miltiades . . . privatus, *lit.*, ' Miltiades having been much engaged (versatus) in important and powerful positions, did not seem to be able to be a private citizen '.

Note that Latin uses videor, ' I seem ', personally, where we prefer to use it impersonally. (The reading of the text, magnis, is an error for (magistratibus.)

l. 143. omnes . . . annos, ' all the years that he had lived there '.

l. 145. **sed iustus**, ' but (he was) a just one '.

l. 147. **omnes . . . qui**, ' all those who '.

l. 149. **usa est**, ' has enjoyed '.

l. 150. **cum . . . tum**, ' not only . . . but also '.

l. 151. **cui . . . pateret**, ' for whom access to him was not open '.

l. 154. **haec populus respiciens**, ' the nation (though) it had regard to this '.

l. 155. **diutius**, ' (any) longer '.

CAESAR

Curio in Africa

The following selection from Caesar is taken from his *Bellum Civile*, Book ii, and comprises Chapters 36-44 of that work. It is the account of one of the battles of the great civil war between Caesar and Pompey, and is of interest inasmuch as it records almost the only phase of those operations in which Caesar's partisans experienced serious defeat, a reverse which is to be accounted for by the too sanguine temperament of Caesar's friend and lieutenant, Curio, as portrayed in these chapters.

A slight sketch of the course of the civil war prior to this battle may be given here, and will prove helpful to an understanding of the text.

Caesar, entering Italy with veteran soldiers from his campaigns in Gaul, had encountered no serious resistance in his home country. Pompey, unable for the present to oppose his rival, had withdrawn across the Adriatic, and some of his troops in Italy, having surrendered to Caesar, had been incorporated in the latter's army. These men later formed part of Curio's force in Africa, and their uncertain loyalty caused their general and his officers much uneasiness.

Caesar, failing for lack of ships to pursue the retreating Pompey across the Adriatic, had gone to Rome, and had brought some order into the chaos there reigning. He had then marched by way of the Riviera into Spain, at that time held by strong Pompeian forces, leaving a portion of his own to invest the city of Massilia (Marseilles) which declared for his rival. In Spain he soon succeeded in defeating Pompey's armies at Ilerda.

Meanwhile Caesarian forces had occupied Sicily, and it was from that island that Curio brought to Africa, intent on winning that province from the Pompeians, the troops that were destined to meet there the harsh fate that this narrative describes, a fate the more striking and tragic in that in all the previous encounters of his short campaign Curio had been uniformly successful.

CHAPTER 36

Line 156. Postero die. The ablative case without a preposition is used to indicate the *point of time* at which something occurs.

l. 156. Curio. Caius Scribonius Curio was a young Roman of good family who had espoused Caesar's cause before the outbreak of the civil war, and had served him well in his political aims. Unfortunately he was less well qualified to win success in the field, being by nature over-confident. This trait, recognized by his friend Caesar, had led to his bringing to Africa forces inadequate to attain his object.

l. 156. Uticam. Utica was a city of the Roman province of Africa, situated on the coast to the north and west of Carthage. It was held at this time by a Pompeian force under the command of P. Attius Varus.

l. 156. vallo circummunire. This task was a usual feature of Roman siege operations and was undertaken of course for the two-fold purpose of ensuring that no supplies reached the beleaguered town and of thwarting sorties on the part of its garrison.

l. 158. **belli.** The genitive depends on **insolens,** which regularly governs this case.

l. 158. **diuturnitate,** ablative of cause, ' owing to the long continuance '.

l. 158. **Uticenses,** i.e., the native African population of the city.

l. 159. **illi,** dative case. Caesar is meant.

l. 159. **conventus.** The word here denotes the Roman, as opposed to the native inhabitants of the city. Translate : ' the Roman population '.

l. 160. **is, qui,** ' (was) such that '. A **qui** clause following upon **is** meaning ' such ' has its verb, as here, in the subjunctive mood, and the use is called generic.

l. 160. **generibus,** ' classes '. The fact that the Romans in the city were thus mixed would mean that a proportion at least would be in sympathy with Caesar and would therefore favour surrender to Curio.

l. 161. **proeliis.** In these previous encounters Curio had been uniformly victorious.

l. 162. **loquebantur,** ' began to talk ', a not uncommon meaning of the imperfect tense.

l. 163. **agebant. agere cum aliquo is** ' to make overtures to '.

l. 163. **pertinacia,** ablative.

l. 164. **vellet,** subjunctive in indirect petition.

l. 164. **agerentur.** The conjunction **cum,** in the meaning ' when ', takes the subjunctive mood when it is used with historic tenses.

l. 165. **Iuba.** Juba was ruler of the African kingdom of Numidia, which was subject to Rome, with a territory corresponding roughly to the French province of Algeria. He had family reasons for taking Pompey's side in the civil war and moreover bore a grudge against Curio personally. Later, when by the victory of Thapsus Caesar had reversed the decision reached before Utica, Juba put an end to his own life.

l. 165. **venerunt, qui . . . dicerent.** A ' purpose ' clause, after a verb of motion, is often expressed by the relative **qui** and the subjunctive mood. Hence **qui dicerent** = ' to say '.

l. 167. **hortarentur.** The object is **eos**, ' them ', understood.

l. 167. **quae res.** Notice here two things : first, that Roman writers frequently begin fresh sentences with relatives, and, this being unnatural in English, you should translate by ' this ', not ' which ' ; second, that the word **res** requires to be rendered in a great variety of ways, according to the context. ' News ' is a suitable translation here.

CHAPTER 37

Line 170. **fides fieri non poterat**, *lit.*, ' belief could not be created ', i.e., ' he could not be persuaded of its truth '.

l. 171. **suarum rerum**, ' in his own position ', depending on **fiduciam**.

l. 172. **res secundae**, ' successes '.

l. 175. **auctoribus**, an ablative of the means, ' by '. But we should say ' from '.

l. 175. **minus**, ' less *than* '.

l. 175. **milibus**, abl., instead of the more usual acc.

l. 176. **relictis munitionibus**, ablative absolute. The **munitiones** are the lines of investment which Curio had begun to construct around the city.

l. 177. **castra Cornelia.** This was the name of a position near Utica previously reconnoitred by Curio and judged by him particularly suitable for a camp. It lay upon a promontory of the coast, and was very close to the city of Utica, but separated from it by marshy ground.

l. 177. **huc**, ' hither ', but we should say ' here '.

l. 179. **misit**, ' sent *word* '.

l. 179. **ūti,** a form of **ut,** (that), and not to be confused with **ūti,** pres. infin. of the deponent verb **utor.**

l. 179. **duae legiones,** etc. Curio, under-estimating the enemy's resources, had brought only two of the four legions available in Sicily, and a mere 500 horsemen.

l. 180. **ad bellum ducendum.** bellum ducere is the regular phrase for ' to prolong a war ', ' to delay operations '.

l. 181. **natura, munitione,** etc., ablatives of cause; similarly **multitudine,** l. 184.

l. 186. **suorum,** ' his *officers* '.

CHAPTER 38

Line 188. **rebus.** See note on res, l. 167. Translate here by ' measures '. Rebus and consiliis are in the ablative absolute construction.

l. 189. **Iubam,** subject to restitisse in the acc. and inf. construction.

l. 190. **controversiis Leptitanorum,** ' owing to disputes with the people of Leptis '. controversiis is ablative of cause. Leptis was a city on the African coast.

l. 194. **rem,** ' issue '.

l. 195. **rem,** ' course of action '.

l. 195. **(eum) adiuvat adulescentia.** In translation, turn the sentence round, making **eum** subject, **adiuvat** passive and adulescentia, etc., ablative : ' in approving this course of action he was greatly influenced by . . .'.

l. 196. **superioris temporis.** Translate by an adjective, ' previous '.

l. 197. **rei bene gerendae,** *lit.,* ' of the thing being done well ', i.e., ' in success '.

l. 197. **rebus.** What would be a suitable rendering for res here?

l. 198. **prima nocte,** ' at nightfall ', a common phrase. Cf. **prima luce,** ' at dawn '.

l. 198. **ad castra,** '*against* the camp'. The second **ad** = ' at '.

l. 199. **Bagradam.** The river Bagradas, where Saburra was encamped, enters the sea east of Castra Cornelia. Curio therefore lay between it and the city of Utica.

l. 200. **erat auditum,** ' it had been heard ', i.e., ' he had heard.'

l. 201. **omnibus copiis.** The preposition **cum,** usually employed to denote accompaniment, is commonly omitted in such cases as the present, where units of military force are perhaps regarded as the instruments of their commander's actions. Contrast, however, l. 210.

l. 202. **intervallo,** ' at a distance '.

l. 203. **imprudentes,** ' without foreknowledge '; **inopinantes,** ' without expectation (of their approach) '.

l. 204. **quadam barbara consuetudine,** *lit.,* ' by a certain barbarian custom '. Caesar means, ' according to a custom prevalent among barbarians '.

l. 208. **quo facto.** See note on **quae res,** Chap. 36, l. 167.

l. 209. **revertuntur.** The passive of **reverto** is used as a deponent verb.

Chapter 39

Line 210. **quarta vigilia,** ablative ' of time when '. For **vigilia,** see the note on l. 367.

l. 211. **cohortibus relictis,** abl. abs.

l. 211. **castris praesidio,** both datives : ' for a guard for the camp ', or as we should prefer to say, ' as a guard '. **praesidio** is called dative of purpose, and **castris** dative of advantage. The dative of purpose is found only after verbs of motion and relinquo. Other examples are the datives of the word **subsidium,** ' support ', and **auxilium,** ' help '. Cf. l. 65.

l. 213. **rem gestam,** ' the thing done ', i.e., ' what had occurred '.

l. 214. **praesit**, subjunctive in an indirect question. Curio's actual question was, **quis praeest**?

l. 215. **Reliqua quaerere**, ' to ask the remaining things ', i.e., ' to put the further questions that he should ', such as, for example, the strength, composition and intentions of Saburra's remaining force, and whether he was in fact unsupported by other troops.

l. 215. **studio**, abl. of cause, ' in his eagerness *to* '.

l. 215. **itineris conficiendi** depends on **studio**.

l. 217. **orationem**, ' story '.

l. 217. **cum perfugis**. We should say ' with *that of* the deserters '.

l. 218. **abesse regem**, etc. The acc. and infs. are in apposition to **orationem**.

l. 219. **pares esse**, ' to be equal ', i.e., ' to match '.

l. 221. **ut ... incipiamus**. When, as mentioned in the introduction to this selection, doubt was felt as to the loyalty of his troops, and Curio had sought in a speech to confirm the waverers, he had particularly mentioned, as a possible cause of the disaffection he suspected, the delay in giving the soldiers the rewards that had been promised them.

l. 222. **erant**. The subject is the clause **quae gesserant equites**, ' what the cavalry had achieved ', or better, ' the achievements of the cavalry '.

l. 222. **per se**, ' in themselves '.

l. 225. **conferretur**. See note on **agerentur**, Ch. 36, l. 164.

l. 225. **ipsis**, i.e. the cavalry.

l. 225. **inflatius**, comparative adverb, *lit.*, ' somewhat exaggeratedly ', i.e., ' with exaggerations '.

l. 226. **ut**, ' as ' or ' in the way that '. Note that in this meaning ut is followed by the indicative.

l. 226. **laudibus**, ' triumphs '.

l. 229. **quidquid intercederet temporis**, ' whatever of time intervened ', i.e., ' every moment lost '. **Temporis is an** example of the *partitive* genitive. **Intercederet** is subjunctive because it occurs between **ut** and **videretur**, i.e., the writer's consciousness that the **ut** requires a subjunctive affects the mood of an intervening verb which would normally be in the indicative. This is called ' subjunctive by attraction '.

l. 229. **hoc omne.** There is no need to translate these words, which are superfluous, for **quidquid . . . temporis** is the subject of **videretur.**

l. 231. **non deerant,** ' were not lacking *to* ', i.e., ' abetted '.

l. 232. **quam maxime perterritos,** ' as much as possible demoralized ', i.e., ' in the greatest possible demoralization '.

l. 232. **ex fuga,** ' consequent upon their flight '.

l. 233. **illi,** i.e., the cavalry.

l. 234. **alii alio loco,** ' one after the other ', *lit.*, ' some in one place, others in another '. Notice how this is economically expressed in Latin, a terse language, by the repetition of **alius.**

l. 235. **resistebant,** ' stayed behind '.

l. 235. **Curionem ad spem.** A curious expression : we should say ' damped the ardour of Curio '.

CHAPTER 40

Line 239. **consuerat.** The pluperfect, of which this is a *syncopated* form, of **consuesco,** ' become accustomed ', commonly means ' was accustomed '. Syncopated forms are very common in Latin verbs, and occur through the dropping of a ' v ' and the following vowel. Cf. **amasse** for **amavisse.**

l. 243. **praemissis equitibus,** abl. of cause, 'from his having sent the cavalry on ahead '.

l. 243. **adfore,** fut. inf. of **adsum.**

l. 245. **simulatione timoris,** ' in pretended fear ', *lit.,* ' in a pretence of fear '.

l. 246. referant : The colon, as often, indicates the opening of a passage in reported speech. Translate ' saying that he ' (sese) . . .

l. 246. esset, cognovisset. All clauses dependent upon indirect statements, commands or questions have their verbs in the subjunctive mood.

l. 247. quod . . . imperaturum, ' and would give such orders as he judged the situation to require ', *lit.,* ' and would order what ', etc.

l. 248. ad superiorem . . . opinione, ' his view of the present time being added to his former hope ', i.e., ' his first hopes heightened by his reading of the situation at the moment '.

l. 250. ex superioribus locis. This luring of an enemy from a position of vantage by pretended flight is paralleled by the Norman tactics at the battle of Hastings.

l. 251. quibus. See note on **quae res,** Ch. 36, l. 167.

l. 251 esset progressus. See note on **agerentur,** Ch. 36, l. 164.

l. 252. confecto exercitu, abl. abs.

l. 252. spatio, ' at a distance (from the camp) '.

Chapter 41

Line 258. **militibus** is dative, dependent on **deerat** at the end of the sentence. In translating make **militibus** subject, and render **deest,** ' lack ', **studium** and **virtus,** of course, becoming the objects.

l. 259. ut in both cases is ' though '.

l. 261. hi, i.e. the cavalry.

l. 261. numero, ' in number ', abl. of respect.

l. 262. hi, the two hundred horsemen that remained.

l. 262. quamcumque in. Take these words in reverse order.

l. 265. ab, ' on '.

l. 266. **aversos proterere**, ' to trample (them) down turned away ', i.e., ' to ride them down from the rear '. **aversos** agrees with an **eos** to be supplied, readily understood from **aciem nostram.**

l. 267. **procucurrissent.** The usual perfect of **curro** when compounded is -**curri.** For the mood see note on **agerentur,** Ch. 36, l. 164.

l. 268. **integri.** The adjective gives the reason for what follows, ' *being* fresh '.

l. 269. **recipientes** agrees with **eos,** to be supplied, referring to the Roman soldiers, and object of **circuibant** and **excludebant,** understood. Translate **se recipientes** by a time clause, ' when they tried to return '.

l. 270. **excludebant,** ' *tried to* cut them off.' Both present and imperfect tenses may denote attempted action.

l. 270. **manere,** and the three other infinitives are subjects to **videbatur.** But translate ' it seemed safe neither to . . .'.

l. 271. **casum subire,** ' to take their chance '.

l. 274. **vires.** Parse this word carefully. It has nothing to do with **vir,** 2nd declension.

l. 277. **hi,** i.e. the wounded men.

l. 279. **consuerunt,** ' are wont '. Cf. note on **consuerant,** Ch. 40, l. 239.

l. 280. **parentes suos . . . potuissent :** ' commended their parents, if fortune should prove able to save any . . .', i.e., ' begged those, if any, whom fortune should avail to save, to care for their parents '.

CHAPTER 42

Line 283. **perterritis omnibus,** abl. of cause, ' owing to the general panic '.

l. 284. **ut in miseris rebus,** ' considering his plight '.

l. 285. **esse arbitratus,** ' thinking (it) to be '.

l. 286. **universos,** object of **iubet,** and equal to **omnes.**

l. 286. **eo**, adverb.

l. 287. **hos**, i.e., the hills.

l. 288. **summam desperationem**. We speak of ' the *depths* of despair '.

l. 289. **partim, partim**. Translate these adverbs by ' some' ' others '.

l. 293. **fuga**, ' in flight '.

l. 293. **petat . . . contendat**, indirect command. Render by infinitives.

l. 294. **se . . . discessurum (esse)** depends on **pollicetur**.

ll. 295.-297. Order for translation : **confirmat se nun-quam reversurum (esse) in eius conspectum, amisso exercitu quem acceperit commissum fidei suae a Caesare.**

l. 295. **amisso exercitu**, abl. abs., ' now that he had lost the army '.

l. 296. **acceperit**. For the mood see note on **esset** and **cognovisset**, Ch. 40, l. 246, and cf. **potuerint**, Ch. 39, l. 220.

l. 299. **quos . . . demonstratum est** : ' who, (as) it has been remarked, had stayed behind '.

l. 299. **equorum reficiendorum** depends on **causa**, ' for the sake of ', *or better*, ' in order to '. See the note on l. 343.

l. 300. **fuga animadversa**, abl. abs.

l. 302. **milites**, i.e., ' the infantry '.

Chapter 43

Line 303. **quaestor**. The duties of officers of this rank were both financial and military. Thus they were not only paymasters and quartermasters, but they also ranked next to the commander-in-chief and had general control over the legions in the field.

l. 304. **suos**, sc. **milites**.

l. 304. **ne deficiant**, indirect petition, ' not to . . .'. Similar are the constructions of **reportentur** and **habeant**, following.

l. 304. animo, abl. of respect, ' in courage '.

l. 307. primo vespere, abl. of time when. ' In the first evening ' =' at dusk '.

l. 308. omnium. Translate ' universal '.

l. 309. alii ... alii ... alii .., ' some . . . others ... others . . .'.

l. 309. dicerent, suspicarentur. These are consecutive (result) subjunctives.

l. 309. adesse copias. This, together with **instare Varum** and **se cernere**, is acc. and inf. dependent on **dicerent**.

l. 313. perterritis omnibus, cf. Ch. 42, l. 283.

l. 313. sibi consulebat. Note that consulo+acc. =' consult '; + dat., ' consult the interests of '.

l. 314. qui, as often, =ei qui, ' those who '.

l. 316. pauci, ' *only* a few '.

l. 316. ad officium imperiumque, ' to their duty and command ', a way of saying ' for the task they had been ordered to carry out '.

l. 318. qui conscenderent, ' *as to* who should embark '.

l. 319. multitudine atque onere, we should say 'by weight of numbers.' Notice how two nouns in parallel construction are thus used to express an idea which in English requires one noun to be subordinate to the other, or even, as in **officium imperiumque** above, l. 316, demands a clause where Latin is content with the second noun.

l. 320. hoc timore, abl. of cause, ' through this fear ', i.e., ' through fear of this '.

CHAPTER 44

Line 322. quibus rebus accidit, ' owing to which circumstances it happened ', i.e., ' the result was '. **pervenirent** is consecutive subjunctive.

l. 322. patres familiae, ' civilians ', doubtless sympathisers with the cause of Caesar.

l. 323. **valerent, possent,** probably generic subjunctives, which involves translating qui ' such as '.

l. 323. **gratia aut misericordia,** abls. of cause, ' through favour or compassion '. The meaning is that some were chosen by the sailors in the boats from being known to and popular among them, others because the rescuers' hearts were touched by piteous appeals.

l. 324. **recepti pervenirent,** ' were taken on board and came '. It is usual in Latin, where two verbs belong to a single subject, for the first to be in the form of a participle.

l. 325. **missis centurionibus,** abl. abs.

l. 326. **numero,** ' as ', with **legatorum,** ' spokesmen ', depending on it.

l. 327. **quarum.** See note on **quae res,** Ch. 36, l. 167.

l. 327. **milites** is object of **conspicatus,** which agrees with **Iuba.**

l. 328. **suam esse praedam.** Supply **eos** as subject to **esse.**

l. 330. **cum Varus ... quereretur ... auderet.** Best render the clauses by participles in the nominative absolute construction : ' Varus complaining . . . but not **(neque)** daring '.

l. 332. **Ipse,** i.e., Juba.

l. 332. **vectus,** ' carried ', but the regular Latin for ' riding '.

l. 332. **prosequentibus,** etc., *lit.,* ' several senators attending : ' but translate : ' attended by several senators ', abl. abs. Caesar is indignant at the shameful thought of a subject princeling's daring to issue orders in a Roman province, with the consent of members of the senate.

l. 336 **post,** adverb, ' later '.

SALLUST

The Surrender of Jugurtha to the Roman Quaestor, Sulla [1]

CHAPTER 105

Line 339. cuius arbitratu . . . consuleretur, *lit.*, ' that by his mediation regard should be had to their common interests '.

Note : (i) cuius = et eius. (ii) consuleretur, a good example of an intransitive verb, used impersonally in the passive.

l. 341. missus ; supply est. The omission of parts of the verb sum is a typical feature of Sulla's fondness for brevity.

l. 342. Balearium, genitive plural in agreement with funditorum. The natives of the Balearic islands in the Mediterranean were celebrated as slingers. It is interesting to note that the modern names Majorca and Minorca are derived from the epithets Major and Minor which were used by the ancients to distinguish them.

l. 343. Paeligna, ' Pelignian '. The Peligni lived in Samnium (Central Italy) and were a hardy and sturdy people. They are equipped here as light-armed troops.

l. 343. itineris properandi causa, ' for the sake of the journey to-be-accelerated ', i.e., ' for the sake of accelerating their journey '.

Note : (i) causa, following its case (genitive), (ii) the gerundive construction, which, in the genitive, is an alternative expression to the gerund with a direct object.

l. 344. denique, ' only '.

l. 345. non amplius, ' not more than '. Note that amplius is not followed by quam or by the ablative of comparison. Equitibus (abl.) is dependent on cum.

[1] For the duties of a quaestor, see the note on Caesar, Chap. 43, l. 303.

l. 346. **Sullae aliisque omnibus,** dative, indirect object of **efficiebant.** The latter has two direct objects and means with the first ' made . . . seem ', and with the second ' produced '. This is a good example of what is known as zeugma.[1] Cf. the English, ' He took his hat and his leave '.

l. 348. **hostilem metum,** ' fear such as an enemy would cause '.

l. 349. **expedire . . . temptare . . . intendere,** historic infinitives, very common in the historians. Translate by an English past tense.

l. 350. **timor . . . quos saepe vicerant.** ' (There was) considerable fear but greater hopes (to them), as victors and against those whom they had often defeated '. Note : (i) the omission of **erat.** (ii) **eis** has to be supplied.

Translate : ' They experienced considerable fear, yet had greater hopes, for they were victorious and (would be fighting) against those whom . . .'.

l. 352. **exploratum,** accusative of the supine, which is often used to express purpose after verbs of motion.

l. 352. **praemissi.** The participle agrees with **equites** and has **exploratum** dependent upon it.

l. 352. **uti erat,** ' as indeed it was '.

l. 353. **nuntiant.** Historic present. Translate by a past tense.

Chapter 106

l. 355. **praesidio,** *lit.,* ' for a protection ', dative of purpose, ' to protect them '.

l. 356. **missum.** Supply esse.

l. 356. **eum et proximum diem,** accusative of time throughout which, ' during that day and the next '.

l. 357. **post,** adverb, ' afterwards '.

l. 357. **locata.** Supply sunt.

l. 357. **diei,** partitive genitive.

[1] A Greek word meaning ' a link ' or ' bond '.

l. 360. **cognitum**, perfect participle passive in agreement with **Iugurtham**. Translate it as if it were **cognitum esse** and supply **et** before **haud procul abesse**.

l. 361. **uti . . . profugeret rogat atque hortatur.** Note that the historic present (as also the historic infinitive) is often followed by historic sequence.

l. 362. **negat se . . . pertimescere**, ' said that . . . he did not fear '.

l. 362. **fusum**, in agreement with **Numidam**. The latter is Jugurtha.

l. 363. **virtuti . . . satis credere.** Indirect speech. ' He had sufficient confidence in the valour of his men '.

l. 366. **cenatos esse**, *lit.*, ' to have had their supper ', =' to get their supper over '. **Ceno** (1), ' I dine ', has a perfect participle, passive in form, that is active in meaning, i.e., **cenatus** =' having dined or supped '.

l. 366. **ignes quam creberrimos**, ' as numerous fires as possible '. Note **quam** + superlative adjective or adverb, ' as . . . as possible '. Sulla ordered his men to leave fires burning in order that the enemy might believe they were still there.

l. 367. **prima vigilia**, ' at the first watch '. The night was divided by the Romans into four ' watches ', which varied in length according to the time of the year, being shorter in summer and longer in winter.

l. 368. **fessis omnibus**, ablative of attendant circumstances or ablative absolute. Translate by a ' while ' clause.

l. 368. **pariter cum ortu solis**, ' at the same time with sunrise ' =' at sunrise '.

l. 369. **cum equites Mauri nuntiant.** A good example of what is known as the ' inverse ' cum construction ; i.e., instead of a ' when ' clause fixing the time for the principal clause, the functions of the two clauses are reversed, and the principal clause merely fixes the time for the action of the ' when ' clause.

l. 370. **duum milium. Supply passuum.**

l. 370. **intervallo.** See l. 202.

l. 371. **quod,** ' which ', connecting relative. Translate by ' and this '.

l. 372. **credere,** historic infinitive, ' they believed '.

l. 373. **proditos . . . circumventos.** Supply **esse** with both verbs.

l. 374. **fuere qui dicerent,** *lit.,* ' there were (some of such a kind) that they said ' = ' some said '. Note the consecutive (result) subjunctive in this phrase ; for **qui** = **ut ei.**

l. 374. **vindicandum . . . relinquendum.** Supply **esse** with both verbs. *Lit.,* ' (that) there was to be a punishing by force and so great a crime on his part (apud illum) was not to be left unavenged '. Translate : ' (that) they should punish him . . . and not leave unavenged . . .'.

Note first that the gerundive expresses ' ought ', ' must ', ' should '—a use confined to the nominative case (accusative also in indirect speech, as here), and secondly that with intransitive verbs the *neuter* of the gerundive is used, with transitive ones the gerundive is used in agreement with its subject. Thus, in this passage, **vindicandum** is neuter, for the verb is used intransitively, but **relinquendum** is in agreement with **scelus.**

Chapter 107

Line 377. **prohibet,** ' defended '.

l. 377. **hortatur . . . gererent.** See the note on Chap. 106, l. 361.

l. 378. **saepe . . . pugnatum,** indirect speech.

l. 379. **pugnatum (esse)** ; this is the infinitive of **pugnatum est,** *lit.,* ' it was fought '. Latin is fond of using intransitive verbs in the passive, but only *impersonally,* i.e., in the third person without a personal subject. English prefers to say ' a successful (bene) battle had been fought '.

l. 380. **quoniam . . . faceret,** ' since, as Sulla thought, he was acting '. Note the subjunctive mood, due to virtual *oratio obliqua,* and how the English translation shows this.

ll. 380-382. **Volucem . . . iubet.** Order for translation : obtestatus Iovem maximum ut adesset testis sceleris atque perfidiae Bocchi, iubet Volucem ex castris abire quoniam hostilia faceret.

l. 383. **orare,** historic infinitive.

l. 383. **nihil . . . factum (esse) . . . ;** indirect speech.

l. 384. **magis calliditate Iugurthae.** Supply **factum esse** from the preceding **factum.**

ll. 385-391. **Ceterum . . . iturum.** The whole of this passage is also in indirect speech. Hence all subordinate clauses have their verb in the subjunctive mood.

l. 387. **eius,** i.e. of Iugurtha.

l. 387. **ex patre suo,** i.e. of Volux. Bocchus, father of Volux, had obviously been a very useful ally to Jugurtha in his fighting against the Romans.

l. 389. **optimum factu,** ' best in the doing ', = ' the best thing to do '. Note the ablative of the supine (ablative of respect), most commonly found with adjectives.

l. 392. **uti in tali negotio,** ' as (the only one) in such a difficulty '.

l. 392. **probata.** Supply **est.**

l. 393. **acciderant,** ' they came upon (him)'.

l. 393. **dubio atque haesitante Iugurtha,** ablative of attendant circumstances or ablative absolute, ' while Jugurtha was uncertain and . . .'.

l. 395. **perventum est,** ' they arrived '. See the note on l. 379 above.

Chapter 108

Line 396. **cum Boccho . . . multum et familiariter agebat,** was constantly conferring with Bocchus on friendly terms '.

l. 399. **orator et . . . speculatum.** Note the variety of expression (combination of noun and supine), which is typical of Sallust's style. *Lit.* ' a negotiator and . . . to discover '. Translate, ' both to negotiate and to discover '.

l. 400. **Mauro,** dative case and referring to Bocchus.

l. 403. **nuntiatum,** accusative of the supine expressing purpose. Cf. **speculatum** above.

l. 404. **colloquio . . . pertimesceret.** Indirect command : ' (that) he (i.e. Sulla) should choose . . . and not be afraid of . . .'.

l. 406. **consulto . . . nequivisse,** indirect speech continued ; *lit.* ' he purposely had everything unbroken with him (i.e. Jugurtha) that their common purpose might be achieved more freely. For otherwise precautions could not have been taken against his treachery '.

Note : (i) **quo** introducing a purpose clause which contains a comparative. (ii) **caveri,** a good example of an intransitive verb used impersonally in the passive. (iii) **consulto . . . habere** might be rendered, ' he had purposely not broken with Jugurtha '.

It will be seen from what follows that there are to be two meetings. At the first one, Jugurtha's envoy, Aspar, is to be present and Bocchus and Sulla will discuss merely formal matters, and thus remove any possible suspicion from Aspar's mind. Then at a second and secret interview Bocchus and Sulla are to discuss the real purpose of their meeting, viz. the surrender of Jugurtha.

l. 407. **res communis,** i.e. the common purpose of Bocchus and Sulla.

l. 409. **Punica fide,** ablative of cause, ' from perfidy '. The origin of **Punica fides** (*lit.* ' Punic faith ', =' utter faithlessness ' or ' perfidy ') seems to date from the days of the Second Punic War, when Hannibal invaded Italy and remained unbeaten for sixteen years 218-202 B.C. Thus, perhaps, it is not surprising that Roman historians and writers blackened Hannibal's character unfairly. This quality of faithlessness was attributed to the Carthaginians and kindred peoples in general. Cf. the history of the modern expressions ' perfidious Albion ' and ' French leave '.

The incident, however, in this extract from Sallust's

Jugurtha will remind us of the English proverb, ' people who live in glass houses should not throw stones '.

l. 410. spe pacis attinuisse, ' kept in hopes of peace '.

l. 412. solitum. Supply esse. Remember that soleo, -ere, ' I am accustomed ', is semi-deponent.

l. 412. Iugurtham . . . traderet, ' whether to betray Jugurtha to the Romans or Sulla to him '.

l. 413. libidinem . . . suasisse, indirect speech, ' personal inclination argued against us, (but) fear for us '.

CHAPTER 109

Line 414. pauca se . . . locuturum, cetera . . . praesentibus, ' that he would say a few things in front of Aspar,[1] (but) the rest (he would discuss) in secret with no witness or the fewest possible present '.

l. 416. quae sibi responderentur, ' what must be said in reply by him ' (i.e. by Bocchus). Responderentur is indirect deliberative subjunctive : the direct form would be quae respondeantur, ' what is to be said in reply '.

l. 417. congressi. Supply sunt.

l. 418. quaesitum, accusative of the supine expressing purpose.

l. 418. pacem . . . foret, ' (whether) he would resolve on peace or war '. Note : (i) the omission of utrum, ' whether '. (i) agitaturus foret, periphrastic future subjunctive (future participle + sim or essem, forem).

l. 419. uti praeceptum fuerat, ' as it had been instructed (to him) ' ; i.e. ' as he had been instructed '. Note that praecipio, being an intransitive verb, can be used only impersonally in the passive.

l. 420. iubet, ' told '.

l. 420. ac . . . responsurum esse. Supply ' said ' after ac.

---

[1] *i.e.* at the first and purely formal meeting, which is described in ll. 417-421.

l. 422. **ambo,** i.e. Sulla and Bocchus. Everything so far has gone according to plan. At this meeting (the first one), which Sallust has just described, there were present Bocchus, Aspar and Sulla. The latter asked Bocchus whether he meant peace or war, to which he gave the pre-arranged answer (**quae sibi responderentur,** l. 416), ' come back in ten days' time '. The next few lines describe the second and secret meeting between Sulla and Bocchus.

l. 423. **plerumque noctis.** Note the partitive genitive.

l. 426. **sanctus vir . . . ambobus,** ' an upright man, approved by both '.

CHAPTER 110

Line 428. **nunquam ego ratus sum fore uti . . . deberem,** ' I never thought that it would be that . . . I might owe ', = ' I never thought that . . . I should owe '. **Fore ut (uti)** + subjunctive mood is sometimes used for the commoner future infinitive. This periphrasis *must* be used with verbs which have no supine and therefore no future infinitive.

l. 431. **ante te cognitum,** ' before you having been known ', = ' before I knew you '.

l. 432. **nullius indigus,** ' though I need no-one's (help) '.

l. 432. **id,** ' my independence ', to which Bocchus has just referred.

l. 432. **id imminutum,** ' my independence lessened ' = ' the loss of my independence '. The phrase is the direct object of **laetor.**

l. 433. **fuerit . . . amicitiae ; eguisse aliquando,** ' to have needed (help) at last ' is the subject of **fuerit.** The latter is perfect subjunctive (iussive) and **pretium** is the complement : *lit.* ' let to have needed (help) at last be for me the price of your friendship '.

l. 434. **qua,** ablative of comparison, ' than which '.

l. 435. **id . . . licet,** ' it is allowed (to you) to make trial of this ', = ' you may make trial of this '. **Adeo** is emphatic, as often with pronouns.

l. 437. **utere**, imperative of utor.

l. 437. **nunquam . . . putaveris**, ' never think that your kindness has been repaid to you '. Note the perfect subjunctive in a negative command, second person, (prohibition), instead of noli (nolite) with the present infinitive.

l. 439. **integra**, ' fresh '. The subject of **erit** is **gratia** (understood).

l. 439. **me sciente**, ' me knowing ', ablative absolute. ' To my knowledge '. Cf. me consule, ' in my consulship '.

l. 441. **paucis accipe**, ' hear in few (words) '. Supply as object ' what I have to say '.

l. 444. **Id omitto**, ' I give this up ', i.e. armed hostilities.

l. 444. **quando**, ' since '.

l. 445. **flumen Muluccham non egrediar . . . sinam**, ' I shall not pass the R. Muluccha nor allow Jugurtha to cross it.' Bocchus means that the R. Muluccha will be the boundary of his territory on the east.

Chapter III

l. 449. **pro se**, ' on his own behalf ', i.e. in reply to Bocchus' compliment.

l. 449. **breviter et modice . . . disseruit**. Supply ' replied ' after modice and ' but ' before de pace. The omission of a conjunction [1] where clauses or phrases are contrasted is very characteristic of Latin.

l. 450. **multis**, ' at length '. verbis is to be understood.

l. 451. **quod polliceretur . . . habituros.** Order for translation (indirect speech) senatum et populum Romanum non habituros in gratiam quod polliceretur, quoniam . . . valuisset.

non in gratiam habituros, ' would not regard as a favour '.

quod polliceretur, ' his promising ', direct object of habituros.

---

[1] Known as asyndeton.

l. 453. **faciendum ... videretur,** *lit.* ' something was to be done by him which seemed to be more to the Roman advantage than his own '.

Note : (i) the gerundive **faciendum,** for which see the note on Ch. 106, l. 374 above. (ii) the impersonal verb **refert,**[1] ' it is of advantage to ', which is followed normally by the genitive (**illorum**), but, instead of the genitive of personal pronouns, by the ablative singular feminine of the possessive adjective (**sua**).

l. 455. **in promptu,** ' easy '.

l. 456. **copiam Iugurthae,** ' access to Jugurtha '.

l. 457. **fore ut ... deberetur,** *lit.* ' it would be that very much would be owed to him ', i.e. ' very much would be owed to him '. For **fore ut,** see the note on l. 428 above.

l. 459. **ultro adventuram (esse),** ' would readily come to him.'

l. 459. **negitare,** historic infinitive.

l. 460. **cognationem ... intervenisse.** Indirect speech. Supply ' he said '.

l. 460. **cognationem, adfinitatem.** The first word implies relationship by blood, the second relationship by marriage, especially between father-in-law and son-in-law. As far as we know there was no immediate blood tie between Bocchus and Jugurtha, but Jugurtha had married a daughter of Bocchus.

l. 461. **intervenisse,** ' formed a connection between them '.

l. 462. **ex,** ' in accordance with '.

l. 463. **ad simulandam pacem,** *lit.* ' for peace to be feigned ' =' for feigning peace ' or ' to feign peace '. We must take this phrase to mean, to give Jugurtha the impression that genuine peace negotiations were being sponsored by Bocchus.

l. 464. **Numida,** i.e. Jugurtha.

l. 465. **quae utilia visa.** Supply **sunt.**

---

[1] In the text **retulisse,** infinitive, dependent on **videretur.**

CHAPTER 112

Line 468. **dicit . . . poni**, ' and told (him) that it had been learned by him (**sibi**) through Dabar from Sulla that war could be ended on (certain) conditions '.

Note : (i) **cognitum** = cognitum esse. (ii) **sibi**, dative of the agent. (iii) **poni** = deponi, *lit.* ' to be laid aside '.

Translate : ' and told him that he had learned through Dabar ', etc.

l. 470. **exquireret**, indirect command, ' he should inquire '.

l. 472. **cuncta edoctus**, ' instructed (in) everything ', = ' having received full instructions '.

l. 475. **saepe antea . . . fuisse**. Indirect Speech continued.

l. 476. **pacem conventam**, ' a peace agreed upon *or* concluded '.

The whole sentence is a sarcastic reference to an earlier incident in the campaign. Four years before the events now being related, Jugurtha had completely defeated a Roman general and imposed severe terms on him and his army, viz. to surrender ignominiously and to quit Numidia within ten days. The senate in Rome refused, however, to ratify the treaty.

l. 476. **ceterum Bocchus . . . vellet**, ' but if Bocchus wished the interests of both to be consulted and (to have) an established peace '. Note : (i) **consultum**, neuter of the perfect participle passive. (ii) **ambobus** (i.e. Jugurtha and Bocchus), dative (indirect object) after **consultum**.

l. 477. **daret operam ut**, ' he should see to it that ', indirect command.

l. 478. **ut una ab omnibus . . . veniretur**, *lit.* ' that there should be a coming together by all ', i.e. ' that all should come together '.

l. 489. **tum fore ut . . . foedus fieret**, ' then it would be that a treaty be made ', i.e. ' then a treaty would be made '. For **fore ut**, see the note on l. 428 above.

l. 481. **neque hominem nobilem ... relictum iri.** Take in
hostium potestate both with non sua ignavia ... publicam
and relictum iri. 'Nor would a man of high rank (who
had fallen) into the hands of the enemy not through his own
fault but in serving his country,[1] be left in their power '.

CHAPTER 113

l. 485. **ceterum dolo ... comperimus.** Supply two words
here : ' whether ' before dolo ; and promiserit, ' he made the
promise', after cunctatus.

l. 486. **in colloquium.** Take with veniretur. The latter
is a good example of an intransitive verb used impersonally
in the passive. See the notes on pugnatum (esse), Ch. 107,
l. 379, and perventum est, Ch. 107, l. 395.

l. 488. **modo ... modo,** ' now ... now '.

l. 488. **appellare ... habere ... polliceri,** historic infinitives.

l. 490. **proxima ... ante diem,** ' preceding the day '.

l. 491. **adhibitis ... remotis,** ' summoning his friends,
and, immediately changing his mind, sending them away '.

l. 493. **vultu ... varius,** *lit.* ' changing in his countenance
and looks in the same way as (pariter atque) in his purpose '.

l. 495. **ex,** ' according to '.

l. 498. **quaestore nostro,** i.e. Sulla, who was quaestor in
the Roman army of Marius. The quaestor was paymaster-
general and acted as the general's second in command.

l. 498. **quasi obvius honoris causa,** ' as if to meet him and
do him honour '. *Lit.* ' for the sake of honour '.

l. 500. **eodem,** adverb, ' to the same spot '.

l. 502. **invaditur,** ' the attack was made *or* they attacked '.

l. 503. **ceteri,** i.e. the necessarii of l. 501.

[1] *Lit.,* ' on account of his country.'

LIVY

How Horatius kept the Bridge

Line 507. alia . . . alia, *n. pl.*, ' some parts . . . others '.

l. 507. Tiberi obiecto, *lit.* ' by the Tiber thrown in the way of the enemy ', i.e. ' by the barrier of the Tiber '.

l. 508. pons sublicius. The ' bridge of piles ', which was for a long time the only bridge over the Tiber, gave access to the city from the Janiculum hill.

l. 508. iter . . . dedit, ni . . . fuisset, ' almost gave a passage (and would have done so) had not there been . . .'. Note the necessity to supply the true apodosis, translated in brackets, to the protasis ni . . . fuisset.

l. 509. Cocles, ' One-eyed '. This name does not necessarily mean that Horatius had only one eye.

l. 509. id munimentum, direct object of habuit, ' that protection ', =' him as a protection '.

l. 515. deum, genitive plural.

l. 515. fidem, ' conscience '.

l. 516. deserto praesidio, abl. abs., ' their post deserted '; translate by an ' if ' clause, i.e. ' if they deserted ' etc.

l. 516. si transitum . . . fore. This sentence is in indirect speech. Supply ' he said '. si transitum pontem reliquissent, ' if they crossed and abandoned the bridge '; cf. nuntium captum interfecerunt, ' they captured and killed the messenger '.

l. 517. plus hostium, ' more (of the) enemy '. Note the partitive genitive which is frequently found after neuter adjectives denoting amount.

l. 519. monere, praedicere. Historic infinitives, to be translated as perfect indicatives. Their commonest use is to describe events which, as here, move rapidly.

The historic infinitive is usually followed by historic sequence, but Caesar and Livy so vary the sequence in indirect or reported speech, that sometimes they maintain the strict sequence as illustrated by Cicero, and sometimes introduce primary tenses even among other verbs which are historic. For a good example, compare the following lines where we have possint, interrumpant and posset.

l. 521. quantum corpore uno posset obsisti, 'as far as resistance could be offered by one person '.

quantum, accusative of extent or adverbial accusative.

posset obsisti, *lit.*, ' it could be resisted '.

l. 523. inter conspecta ... arma ; conspecta agrees with terga, and pugna is abl. with cedentium, ' of (those) withdrawing from the fight '.

l. 524. ad ineundum proelium, ' for the battle to-be-begun ', i.e. ' for beginning the battle '. ineundum, neut. acc. of the gerundive in agreement with proelium.

l. 528. quod ... erat, ' what was the most stormy moment of the fight ', direct object (with procellam) of sustinuit.

l. 530. revocantibus qui rescindebant ; the antecedent of qui is the pronoun illis (understood).

l. 532. circumferens ... oculos ad, ' whirling (i.e. darting) fierce looks threateningly at '.

l. 533. provocare, increpare ; historic infinitives. See the note on l. 519 above.

l. 534. servitia ... venire, indirect speech dependent on a verb of saying which can easily be supplied from increpare. servitia, ' tools '; oppugnatum, accusative of the supine expressing purpose.

l. 536. dum alius alium ... circumspectant, ' while one looked at another ', i.e. ' while they looked at one another '.

l. 539. quae cum, ' which when ', = ' when they '. Latin often connects sentences together in this way, i.e. by means of the relative pronoun referring to some person or thing in the previous sentence. Quae here refers of course to tela.

l. 540. neque ille minus obstinatus, ' and yet he none the less firmly '.

l. 542. **cum simul fragor . . . sustinuit.** Note this example of what is called the inverse-cum-construction which is always followed by the indicative mood. Cf. **Discesserat Hilarus cum venit tabellarius,** ' Hilarus had just departed when the letter-carrier arrived '. Read again the note on l. 369.

l. 543. **alacritate perfecti operis sublatus,** ' (the shout) raised in their glee at the completion of their task (*lit.* of their task having been completed).'

l. 545. **inquit.** Note : (i) that **inquit** is used for ' he said ' when the actual words of the speaker are quoted (Direct Speech) ; (ii) that is is placed second or third word in the sentence, never first.

l. 545. **sancte,** adverb. **Precor . . . accipias,** ' I pray (that) you receive '. Note the omission of **ut.**

l. 546. **propitio flumine,** ' with favouring stream '.

l. 547. **ita,** ' thereon '. **sic armatus,** ' so armed ' = ' armed as he was '.

l. 548. **multis superincidentibus armis,** ' many missiles falling about and around him ', = ' though many missiles fell around him '.

l. 549. **rem . . . fidei,** ' having dared a deed destined to win (**habituram**) more fame than credence with posterity '. Note : (i) **ausus,** perfect participle of the semi-deponent **audeo.** (ii) **rem ausus** = ' having performed a daring deed '. (iii) **habituram,** future participle active. (iv) **plus famae quam fidei,** ' more of fame than of credence ', partitive genitives. Cf. the note on l. 516 above.

In his edition, Conway calls this a ' skilfully chosen phrase which neither asserts nor denies Livy's own belief in the story he has so splendidly recorded '.

l. 551. **in comitio,** ' in the comitium '. The latter was an open space used for various assemblies and for the law courts. It lay to the north-east of the forum.

l. 551. **agri quantum . . . datum,** ' as much (of) land as he could plough in a single day, was given (him) '.

Note : (i) **agri,** partitive genitive depending on **quantum.**
(ii) **posita, . . . datum.** Supply **est** with both verbs. Livy
frequently omits the auxiliary verb **esse** in the compound
tenses of the Latin verb.

The Story of Mucius Scaevola

l. 553. **frumenti.** Take this genitive with **inopia.**

l. 554. **sedendoque . . . habebat.** Order for translation :
Porsinna habebat spem = (sperabat) **se expugnaturum
urbem sedendo. sedendo,** 'by sitting ', ='by remaining
encamped '.

l. 557. **quorum . . . fuderit.** Note the tense (*perfect*) and
mood (*subjunctive*) of this relative clause. The mood is due
to the fact that the clause is subordinate in indirect speech.
Finally note that Livy often retains primary tenses in
historic sequence. Cf. the note on Horatius, l. 519.

l. 558. **eam indignitatem . . . ratus,** ' having thought that
that outrage (was) to be avenged ', i.e. ' thinking that he
ought to avenge that outrage '. Note that in the nominative (and also in the accusative in *oratio obliqua*, as here) the
gerundive expresses ' ought ', ' must ', ' should '. Read
again the note on l. 374.

l. 561. **ne . . . forte deprehensus . . . retraheretur ut transfuga,** ' lest . . . he might by chance be caught and dragged
back . . . as a deserter '. Note : (i) Latin has perfect
participle passive and *one* finite verb where English has *two*
finite verbs. (ii) **ut** meaning ' as '.

l. 563. **fortuna .. adfirmante,** ablative absolute. This
construction may be translated into English in a variety of
ways, common ones being adverbial, ' when ', ' after ', ' as ',
' since ', or ' if ' clauses. Here a causal (' as ', ' since ')
clause would be most apt; ' especially as the fortune
of the city would confirm such a charge '.

l. 566. **non praedo nec . . . ultor,** ' not as a freebooter nor
to avenge (**ultor**) their raids in our turn '.

populationum, objective genitive dependent on **ultor,** ' avenger '.

The name objective is given where the relation of the genitive to the noun on which it depends is similar to that between an object and its verb.

l. 570. **tribunal,** in a Roman camp, was a raised platform of turf on the left of the general's tent **(praetorium),** from which he addressed the soldiers.

l. 572. **pari fere ornatu,** ' in much the same sort of dress '.

l. 573. **multa ageret,** ' was doing many things ' = ' was busy '. Cf. **nihil agere,** ' to be idle '.

l. 574. **ne . . . semet aperiret quis esset,** ' lest . . . he himself might disclose himself who he was '. Cf. the New Testament literal translation of what is really a Greek idiom, ' I know thee who thou art '. **esset :** explain the subjunctive.

l. 575. **quo . . . facinus,** ' whither fate by chance led the deed '. Supply some such word as ' following '.

l. 576. **vadentem . . . vocant.** In the translation of this sentence, it would be a help to turn the present participle **vadentem** by a main verb ' he strode ' and insert ' and ' before **cum,** l. 578.

l. 578. **cum . . . retraxissent,** *lit.* ' when a rush having been made at the shout, the king's attendants dragged him back having been seized '. Translate, ' when, rushing towards the shouting, the king's attendants seized and dragged him back '. Cf. the note on Horatius, l. 516.

l. 580. **destitutus,** ' brought forward and placed '.

l. 583. **nec ad mortem . . . ad caedem,** ' and there is no less (of) courage (to me) for death than there was for murder ', i.e. ' I have no less courage ' etc.

l. 584. **et . . . et,** ' both . . . and '.

l. 586. **idem petentium decus,** ' of (men) seeking the same glory '.

l. 587. **accingere.** Second pers. sing. present imperative passive, ' make yourself ready for '.

l. 588. in singulas horas, ' for each hour in turn,' = ' from hour to hour '.

l. 590. iuventus Romana, nominative, ' we, the Roman youth '.

l. 590. nullam aciem . . . timueris. Note the perfect subjunctive here, which expresses a prohibition (negative command). This use is colloquial and is replaced in the written language by noli, nolite + the infinitive.

l. 591. uni, dative singular in agreement with tibi.

l. 592. res, ' the struggle '.

l. 593. ira, ablative with infensus.

l. 594. minitabundus. Translate by an adverb, ' threateningly '.

l. 595. quas . . . iaceret, indirect question, object of expromeret ; ' what threats of treachery he (i.e. Mucius) was hurling in riddles at him (i.e. Porsinna) '.

l. 596. en, 'lo!', 'behold'. tibi, 'for yourself' with sentias.

l. 598. accenso . . . foculo, dative after the compound verb inicit.

l. 599. quam, ' it ' (i.e. his right hand), direct object of torreret, ' allowed to burn '.

l. 599. velut alienato ab sensu . . . animo, ' as if his consciousness (animo) were bereft of feeling '.

l. 600. cum . . . prosiluisset . . . iussisset. Omit the cum and translate the pluperfect subjunctives as if they were perfect indicatives and main verbs. Finally insert ' and ' before inquit.

l. 602. in te . . . ausus, lit., ' having dared hostile actions against yourself rather than against me '.

l. 603. iuberem macte virtute esse, lit. ' I would bid you be blessed with your valour ', i.e. ' I would bid you, " well done " '. macte is probably an adverb.

Note the conditional sentence iuberem . . . si . . . staret ; unreal in present time, imperfect subjunctive.

l. 604. ista virtus, ' such courage as yours '.

l. 605. **iure belli liberum**, ' free from the rights of war ', is in agreement with **te**.   So also is **intactum** and **inviolatum**. The phrase means that Mucius may go free from the power which war gives Porsinna over him.

l. 607. **quando**, ' since '.

l. 608. **ut . . . tuleris**, ' that you may find yourself to have won '.   Note the perfect subjunctive in this purpose clause, representing the action as single or completed.

l. 609. **quod . . . nequisti**, direct object of **tuleris**, ' what . . .'.

l. 612. **ut cuiusque ceciderit primi**, *lit.*, ' as (the lot, sors) of each man next will have fallen '.

l. 613. **suo quisque tempore**. **quisque** is in apposition with the subject **ceteri**, l. 612, ' each in his own time '.

The Gauls march on Rome

l. 615. **Gallos quoque**, ' the Gauls for their part '.

l. 618. **vereri . . . legere . . . coacervare**, historic infinitives. See the note on Horatius, l. 519.

l. 620. **nihil hostile**, ' nothing hostile ', =' no enemy '.

l. 621. **multo**, ablative of the measure of difference, usually found with comparatives or words with a comparative idea.

l. 622. **perveniunt**, historic present.   Translate by a past tense.

l. 622. **ubi**, ' where ', connecting relative adverb.   Translate by ' and there '.

l. 623. **cum praegressi equites . . . rettulissent**, ' when the cavalry who had gone on ahead reported that ' etc.

l. 625. **aliud priori simile miraculum**, ' this second marvel like to the first '.

l. 627. **consedere**=**consederunt**. Livy is fond of the ending -**ēre** in the third pers. pl. perf. indic. act.

l. 628. **aliasque portas**, either ' the gates as well ', or ' the other gates ', i.e. those in addition to the ones they saw when they first approached Rome (cf. l. 624).

l. 629. quaenam ... consilia essent, indirect question depending on the verbal idea contained in exploratoribus. Insert ' to see '.

l. 629. in perdita re, ' in their desperate plight '.

l. 630. Veios petisset. After the Gauls had defeated the Romans at the battle of the Alia, the majority of the Roman fugitives succeeded in escaping safely to Veii, a town about 13 miles north of Rome. The Alia is a small river which flows into the R. Tiber about 10 miles north of Rome. Only those on the Roman right wing retreated on Rome.

l. 632. complorati omnes pariter vivi mortuique, ' all mourned alike whether dead or living '.

l. 634. luctus, acc. plural, direct object of stupefecit. Privatos is in agreement with it.

l. 637. vagantibus ... barbaris, abl., abs., ' as the barbarians ranged around the city-walls in squadrons (of cavalry) '.

l. 638. omne inde tempus, ' all the time from then ', = ' all the intervening time ', nominative case.

l. 639. ut identidem ... impetus, ' that repeatedly the attack seemed likely-to-be (futurus) immediately (iam) against the city '. futurus might also be translated, ' likely to be launched '.

l. 641. mansuros enim ad Aliam fuisse, ' for (they thought that) they would have stayed at the Alia '. Note the indirect speech and the necessity to supply ' they thought '.

l. 642. foret = esset.

l. 643. haud multum diei. Note the partitive genitive and see the note on Horatius, l. 517.

l. 644. dilatum consilium esse, indirect speech. See the note on l. 641 above.

l. 645. quo plus pavoris inferrent, ' in order to inspire more panic '. Note : (i) pavoris—what kind of a genitive ?

(ii) **quo** replaces **ut** in purpose clauses which contain a comparative.

l. 646. **exanimare,** historic infinitive. Supply an object, ' them ' or ' the Romans '.

l. 646. **timorique . . . fuit,** ' and disaster itself followed hard upon (*lit.* was following on) their constant fear '.

l. 649. **ea nocte . . . insequenti die,** ablative of time when.

l. 651. **civitas,** *lit.* ' the state ' = ' the citizens '. Note this use of the abstract where we would prefer the concrete.

l. 651. **nam . . . esset.** Order for translation : **nam cum** (since) **esset nulla spes urbem posse defendi tam parva manu relicta.**

l. 652. **placuit. Placeo,** ' I please ', is often used *impersonally* (i.e. in the 3rd person sing.) in the meaning, ' it is decided, determined upon '. Translate ' they decided '.

l. 653. **iuventutem militarem . . . robur.** Note again the use of the abstract, where we might prefer the concrete, e.g. ' the young men fit for service and the strongest members of the senate '.

Robur literally means ' hard wood ', ' oakwood '. Then it was used figuratively for ' hardness ', ' strength ', ' force ' and finally for ' the best part ', ' the flower '.

l. 654. **in arcem Capitoliumque.** ' The Capitoline hill has two summits with a hollow between : the southern summit was the Capitolium, containing the great national temple, the northern was the citadel of Rome.' Whibley in his edition of Livy, Bk. V.

l. 655. **inde,** ' from there ', is explained by **ex loco munito.**

l. 656. **Romanum nomen,** ' the Roman race '. **Nomen Romanum** signifies all those who bear the name of Roman.

l. 657. **flaminem . . . auferre,** ' (they decided) that the flamen and the Vestal Virgins should carry . . .'.

This flamen (or priest) was the flamen Quirinalis whose duties were particularly connected with the worship of Vesta. The latter was the goddess of the household and hearth, and regarded with the greatest veneration by the Romans.

Her symbol was fire which was kept perpetually burning on her altar by the Vestal Virgins, priestesses who dedicated themselves to the service of the goddess.

l. 658. **nec ante deseri . . . qui colerent.** Order for translation, **cultum deorum nec** (=not) **deseri antequam qui** (those who) **colerent, non superessent).**

Note : (i) **cultum . . . deseri,** is dependent on **placuit,** l. 652. (ii) **deseri** is the present infinitive passive. (iii) the separation in the text of **ante** from **quam,** a common idiom known as tmesis. (iv) the necessity to supply the antecedent of **qui.**

l. 660. **si arx Capitoliumque . . . superfuerit.** Note that although there are three subjects **arx Capitoliumque, senatus,** and **militaris iuventus,** the verb **superfuerit** is in the singular, thus agreeing in number only with the nearest subject. Note also that **sedes deorum** is in apposition with **arx Capitoliumque,** and **caput publici consilii** with **senatus.**

l. 661. **superfuerit imminenti ruinae urbis.** Note : (i) **supersum** ' survive ', is followed by the dative. (ii) **superfuerit** is subjunctive mood (perfect) because the conditional clause is subordinate in indirect speech.

l. 662. **facilem iacturam esse,** ' the sacrifice would be light (they thought) '. Note the indirect speech and that **esse** here is equivalent to **fore,** future infinitive.

l. 663. **seniorum . . . turbae.** Order for translation, **turbae** (genitive dependent on **iacturam**) **seniorum relictae in urbe periturae utique.** Parse **periturae** (from **perire**), carefully.

l. 664. **quo . . . ferret.** See the note on l. 645 above. **Fero** here means ' endure ', ' put up with '.

l. 664. **de plebe multitudo,** ' the mob of the people ', nominative and therefore subject of **ferret.** This rather contemptuous phrase reminds us that Livy's political sympathies favoured the patricians or nobles.

l. 665. **Senes . . . obituros.** Order for translation : **senes triumphales consularesque palam dicere** (historic infinitive) **se obituros** (esse) **simul cum illis.**

senes triumphales consularesque are ' old men who had celebrated a triumph or had held the consulship '. In his edition of the Vth Book, Whibley notes that of the generals who are known to have triumphed within 60 years, there was probably only one then alive.

The triumphus, or public honour decreed to a successful general on his return from a campaign, consisted of a procession along the Via Sacra (Sacred Way) to the Capitolium, where sacrifice was offered to Jupiter. At the head of the procession walked the magistrates and senators, then were dragged on wagons the enemy's spoils, and models depicting scenes in the campaign, then came priests leading white bulls with gilded horns, next the captives and enemy generals, and then the successful general drawn in a chariot by four horses. Finally followed the general's army, cavalry first, and infantry next.

l. 667. quibus . . . possent. Explain the mood of possent. See the note on l. 661 above.

l. 668. inopiam armatorum, ' the want of armed men ' = ' armed men in their want '.

CHAPTER 40

Line 669. haec . . . solacia. Order for translation : haec solacia (sunt) iactata inter seniores destinatos morti. Note the necessity to supply sunt with iactata. See also the next line.

l. 670. Versae inde adhortationes, ' encouragement was then directed '. Versae, supply sunt. Note that Latin often uses abstract nouns in the plural, when they are often best rendered into English by concrete phrases. Here we might translate by ' encouraging words '. Cf. amicitiae = ' friends '.

l. 671. prosequebantur. The subject is the old men.

l. 673. urbis . . . fortuna. quaecumque reliqua esset fortuna is the direct object of commendantes, and has urbis . . . victricis dependent on it. Thus the order for translation is : quaecumque fortuna esset reliqua, urbis victricis omnibus bellis trecentos sexaginta annos.

l. 674. Digredientibus qui . . . ferebant. Note that the subject of the abl. absol. digredientibus is the unexpressed antecedent of qui. ' As those who . . ., departed from those (ab eis, l. 676) who . . .'

l. 677. cum . . . tum, ' not only . . . but also '.

l. 679. nunc hos nunc illos sequentium rogitantiumque, ' (of women) following now these, now those, and repeatedly asking '.

hos, illos, i.e. their husbands who were going to be left behind, and their sons who were going to defend the Capitolium.

l. 680. cui fato, dative, ' to what doom '.

l. 680. nihil . . . relinquebant, ' left nothing in (lit., of) human misfortune that could be added (lit. was left) '.

l. 683. quia quod utile . . . erat, ' because what was expedient to the besieged in reducing the numbers of those unfit for service (imbellem), was hardly human '.

l. 687. ex urbe effusa, ' streaming from the city ', is in agreement with alia maxime plebis turba, ' the rest of the crowd (consisting) mostly of plebeians '.

l. 689. pars . . . pars, ' some . . . others '. Note that the collective noun pars (fem.) has in agreement with it dilapsi (masc. plur.).

l. 689. dilapsi ; supply sunt ; ' scattered '.

l. 691. communibus deploratis, ' despairing of public interest '. Supply rebus with communibus.

Chapter 41

l. 692. Romae, locative case, ' at or in Rome '.

l. 692. omnibus ; supply rebus. See the note on l. 691 above.

l. 692. ut in tali re, ' as (best they could) in such circumstances '.

l. 693. **ad tuendam arcem**, *lit.*, ' for the citadel to-be·defended ', i.e. ' for defending the citadel '. Note that in the accusative case, the gerund with an accusative object is replaced by the gerundive construction, i.e. the object takes the case of the gerund and the gerundive is made to agree with it as an adjective.

l. 693. **turba . . . regressi.** For the agreement of regressi (masc. plur.) with the collective noun turba (fem.), see the note on Ch. 40, l. 689.

l. 695. **qui eorum**, ' those of them who . . .'.

l. 695. **curules . . . magistratus**, *acc. pl.*, ' curule offices ' were those in which the magistrates were entitled to sit in the ivory chair (eburnea sella, l. 699). Only consuls, praetors and curule aediles were given this honour.

l. 696. **in fortunae . . . insignibus**, ' in the regalia of their former rank and office and power '.

l. 698. **quae augustissima . . . ea vestiti**, *lit.*, ' what is the most venerable garment to those leading the chariots (of the gods) or celebrating a triumph, (they) clothed in it '.

Note : (i) the relative clause comes first in Latin, whereas English prefers to have it later. (ii) the antecedent of the relative clause, augustissima vestis, is *inside* the relative clause and attracted from the ablative case to the nominative.[1] We might then translate, ' clothed in the most venerable garment which belongs to those leading the chariots . . .'.

l. 698. **tensas ducentibus.** At the opening of the Circensian games held in the Circus,[2] a procession was held in which images of the gods were carried in sacred chariots (tensae) and attended by the principal magistrates. On this occasion the latter wore the toga picta (or embroidered

---

[1] *i.e.* from the case of the antecedent (ea) to the case of the relative pronoun.

[2] An oval open space between the Palatine and Aventine Hills.

cloak [1]) and the **tunica palmata** (or tunic embroidered with palm twigs). The same decorations were also worn by those who celebrated a triumph.

l. 699. **sedere**, historic infinitive.

l. 701. **patente Collina porta**, abl., ' by the wide-open Colline gate '. This was near the Quirinal Hill.

l. 703. **deum**, genitive plural.

l. 704. **ne quis . . . impetus fieret,** ' that no attack be made '.

l. 706. **dilapsi.** Translate as though it were **dilapsi sunt** and insert ' and ' before the next nominative **pars.**

l. 706. **vacuis occursu hominum viis,** *lit.,* ' in the streets empty from the meeting of men ', i.e. ' in the deserted streets where they met no one '.

l. 707. **in proxima quaeque tectorum,** ' into each nearest of the houses ', i.e. ' into all the nearest houses '. **Quisque** with superlatives and ordinals is loosely equivalent to our ' every ', or ' all '.

l. 708. **velut ea . . . intacta et referta** = velut si . . . intacta **et referta essent. Praeda** is ablative case.

l. 710. **ne qua fraus hostilis,** ' that no enemy ambush . . .'. Cf. l. 704 above.

l. 712. **ubi,** ' where, =' and there '.

l. 712. **haud secus quam venerabundi,** ' not otherwise than with respect ', =' even so with respect '.

l. 713. **praeter,** ' in addition to '.

l. 714. **humano,** ablative of comparison.

l. 714. **maiestate,** ablative of respect, ' in their dignity '. Take with **simillimos.**

l. 715. **ad eos . . . versi,** ' facing them as if (they were) statues '.

l. 716. **M. Papirius . . . movisse,** *lit.,* ' M. Papirius, one of them, is said to have aroused anger to a Gaul stroking

---

[1] The toga, the national dress of the Roman, consisted of plain white wool.

nis beard, having been struck on the head with his ivory
staff '.

Note : (i) The Latin order is the chronological order, i.e.
permulcenti, ' stroking his beard ' ; **in caput incusso**,
' struck on the head ' ; **iram movisse**, ' to have aroused his
anger '. (ii) **Gallo** (with **permulcenti** and **incusso** in agreement) is dative of the person interested, often to be translated by a genitive in English.

Perhaps we might translate : ' M. Papirius, one of them,
is said to have aroused the anger of a Gaul who stroked
his beard, by striking him on the head with his ivory staff '.

l. 717. **scipione eburneo.** The ivory staff, tipped with
gold, was one of the regalia of a magistrate who had celebrated
a triumph.

l. 718. **atque ab eo ... inici ignes.** This sentence is in
indirect speech as though **dixerunt**, not **dicitur**, had pre-
ceded.

l. 719. **ortum, . . . trucidatos.** Supply **esse**.

l. 720. **nulli** (more usually **nemini**), dative of **nemo**,
dependent on **parci**. The latter is the infinitive of **parcitur**.
Note that Latin only uses intransitive verbs impersonally
in the passive. Thus ' no one is spared ' becomes **nulli
(nemini) parcitur**, *lit.*, ' there is a sparing to no-one '.

CICERO

Murder on the Appian Way

SECTION 24

Line 722. **P. Clodius.** Publius Clodius first came into
prominence in 62 B.C. as a result of his profanation of the
rites of the goddess Bona Dea. At his trial the following
year, bribery secured his acquittal, in spite of the fact that
Cicero's evidence disproved his alibi. Hence arose the
beginning of his feud with Cicero.

Clodius held the quaestorship in Sicily in 61 B.C., **and**

became tribune in 58. During this year, as leader of the Popular Party, he secured the banishment of Cicero and ruled Rome with his armed bands of ruffians and slaves.

The next year, however, there arose a rival gangster, Milo, who meeting violence with violence, and armed slaves with armed slaves, secured the recall of Cicero and kept Clodius at bay. During the following years, we hear little of their rival activities, and it is not until the winter of 53 B.C., when Clodius was a candidate for the praetorship, and Milo for the consulship, that the quarrel between the two broke out again. At this point, we may begin Cicero's narrative of the incidents which led up to the scuffle on the Appian Way, in which Clodius was killed.

l. 723. **ita tracta . . . anno superiore,** ' that the elections had been so delayed the year before '.

anno superiore, 54 B.C.

l. 725. **qui . . . spectaret, . . . vellet, . . . quaereret. Qui** is here causal ; hence it is followed by the subjunctive mood : ' inasmuch as he did not look to the degree of his office.'

l. 726. **sed et L. Paulum . . . vellet,** ' but wished to avoid L. Paulus (as) his colleague '.

l. 728. **ad dilacerandam rem publicam,** ' for the state to be torn to pieces ', =' for tearing the state to pieces '. For the gerundive construction, see the note on Livy, ' The Gauls march on Rome ', Ch. 41, l. 693.

l. 729. **annum suum,** ' his (proper) year ', i.e. 53 B.C.

l. 730. **non, ut fit, religione aliqua,** ' not, as is usual, by reason of any religious scruple '. A candidate might have felt some religious scruple if the auspices had been unfavourable at the elections.

l. 731. **quod ipse dicebat,** ' as *he* used to say '.

l. 732. **hoc est,** ' that is (to say) '.

l. 732. **plenum annum atque integrum,** direct object of **haberet,** l. 731.

SECTION 25

Line 734. **occurrebat ei,** ' it occurred to him '.

l. 735. **consule Milone,** ' if Milo were consul ', *lit.*, ' Milo (as) consul ', ablative absolute.

l. 736. **fieri,** ' was likely to become '.

l. 737. **sed ita . . . ut . . . gubernaret,** ' but in such a way that he alone controlled ' etc.

l. 738. **etiam invitis illis,** ' even against their will '; ablative absolute. Cf. **consule Milone,** l. 735 above.

l. 740. **tribus,** i.e. representatives of the tribes. In this way Clodius hoped to persuade leading men of the tribes to lead the voting against Milo. At the annual elections, the tribes voted in order of precedence and recorded a block vote, a majority of the centuries in the tribe deciding whether it was ' in favour ' or ' against '.

l. 740. **quanto ille plura miscebat,** ' by how much he mixed more things ', i.e. ' the more Clodius spread confusion '. Note **quanto** in this use with comparatives, ablative of the measure of difference. It is often answered by **tanto** with a comparative as in l. 741.

l. 741. **hic,** i.e. Milo, who is present in court.

l. 742. **homo ad omne facinus paratissimus,** ' this fellow ready for any crime '.

l. 743. **fortissimum . . . inimicissimum . . . certissimum.** Note Cicero's fondness for superlatives. We might render by, ' a very brave man, his bitterest foe and most certain (to be) consul '.

l. 745. **suffragiis.** The herald declared the block vote of each century [1] or group within the tribe. The total voting of the centuries determined the block vote of the tribe.

l. 747. **occidendum (esse) Milonem,** ' that Milo (was) to be slain ' = ' that Milo must be slain '. Note that the

---

[1] In the **comitia centuriata** (or assembly by centuries), the members of the tribe were grouped in centuries (nominally groups of 100) according to their wealth.

gerundive expresses 'ought', 'must', 'should'. This
use is confined to the nominative case (accusative also when
in indirect speech). See Sallust, Ch. 106, l. 374.

Section 26

Line 748. **servos agrestes et barbaros**, direct object of
deduxerat. It seems that Clodius organised bands of wild
and possibly runaway slaves, and maintained them in a
camp on the Apennine Hills. From this base he pillaged
the public forests in Etruria.

l. 748. **quibus**, instrumental ablative, 'by means of whom'.

l. 752. **Miloni**, dative of disadvantage, 'from Milo'.

l. 752. **vitam posse**, '(but) his life could'. This absence
of a conjunction is typical of Latin which prefers to obtain
contrast by mere apposition of phrases and clauses.

l. 753. **quin etiam**, 'nay, more'.

l. 754. **M. Favonio . . . quaerenti**; the datives depend on
respondit. Translate the participle by a 'when' clause.

l. 754. **M. Favonio, fortissimo viro**. Note how Latin
expresses, 'the brave M. Favonius'. Another example will
help : 'your distinguished father' becomes in Latin **tuus
pater, vir clarissimus**.

l. 755. **qua spe fureret**, *lit.*, 'with what hopes he was
frenzied', i.e. 'what he hoped to get by his frenzy'.

l. 755. **triduo . . . quadriduo**, ablative of time within
which.

l. 756. **summum**, adverb. See the vocabulary.

l. 757. **ad hunc M. Catonem**, 'to M. Cato here', i.e. 'in
court'.

Favonius was a great admirer of the obstinate die-hard
Marcus Cato, and imitated his conduct and character so
servilely that he was nicknamed Cato's ape.

SECTION 27

Line 760. **a Lanuvinis,** ' from the citizens of Lanuvium '. The latter is an ancient town about 25 miles south-east of Rome. It is now called Città Lavinia.

l. 760. **iter sollemne . . . Lanuvium,** *lit.*, ' that the yearly, usual and necessary journey on the 18th January was for Milo to Lanuvium ', i.e. ' that Milo had to make his yearly and usual journey to Lanuvium on the 18th[1] January '.

l. 762. **ad flaminem prodendum,** ' for the priest to be appointed ' = ' for appointing the priest '. As we learn in the next line, Milo was ' dictator ' or chief magistrate in Lanuvium and it was one of his duties to nominate a priest of Juno from a number of privileged persons.

For the gerundive construction, see the note on **ad tuendam arcem,** Livy, ' The Gauls March on Rome ', Ch. 41, l. 693.

l. 763. **Lanuvi,** vocative case.

l. 765. **quod re intellectum est,** ' as was realised by the event '.

l. 765. **ita . . . ut . . . relinqueret,** ' in such circumstances as to throw over '.

l. 768. **quam nisi . . . nunquam reliquisset,** ' which he would never have thrown over, if he had not wanted to be present at the place and the time of his crime '. This is an excellent example of a conditional clause, unreal in past time. Note : (i) the pluperfect subjunctive in both ' if ' clause and main clause. (ii) nisi = ' if not '.

SECTION 28

Line 773. **ut fit,** ' as is often the case '.

l. 774. **id temporis cum . . . potuisset,** ' at such a time that Clodius could have returned, if, that is, he intended to come to Rome on that day '.

[1] Before the reform of the calendar by Caesar, January had only 29 days.

Note : (i) **id temporis**. The partitive genitive is often found after neuter adjectives denoting amount, e.g. **multum temporis**. A similar use is found here after **id**. (ii) **venturus erat**, periphrastic future, ' intended to come '. (iii) **potuisset**, consecutive (result) subjunctive.

l. 776. **ei**, dative case, referring to Milo.

l. 777. **nulla raeda ... comitibus**, ablative of attendant circumstances. The Greek retinue (**Graeci comites**) consisted of jesters and musicians (usually Greek slaves) whom wealthy Romans took with them on journeys to beguile the way.

l. 778. **ut solebat**, ' as he was accustomed '. Translate ' whom he usually took with him '.

l. 779. **sine uxore, quod nunquam fere**, ' without his wife, as almost never '. Supply **fecit** and translate ' and without his wife whom he practically never left behind '.

l. 779. Note the effective way in which Cicero contrasts the appearance of the two travellers : Clodius, on horseback and unencumbered by carriage or retinue ; Milo with his wife and a large train of attendants. And yet Milo's enemies, Cicero points out, declare that it was Milo who had deliberately set out to do murder.

Imagine what your own reaction as a member of the jury would be to this description of the events leading up to the death of Clodius.

l. 779. **cum hic insidiator ... apparasset**, ' while this treacherous bandit here who (they said) had planned that journey to commit murder ...'.

Note : (i) **hic insidiator** refers to Milo. Cicero is using irony. (ii) **qui ... apparasset**. The subjunctive mood shows that this accusation was made by Milo's enemies. Note how the English translation shows this. (iii) **ad caedem faciendam**, cf. l. 762 above and the passage of Livy referred to.

l. 781. **magno et impedito ... comitatu**. What kind of an ablative is this?

Section 29

Line 783. **hora fere undecima,** about 3.30 p.m. The Romans divided the daylight into twelve equal hours, and these would naturally vary in length according to the time of the year. At the time of these events (January), the diurnal hour would be about 45 minutes.

l. 784. **aut non multo secus,** ' or not (by) much otherwise ' = ' or about that '. Note **multo,** ablative of the measure of difference (found chiefly with comparatives or words with a comparative idea).

ll. 785-787. **in hunc, hic.** Note how hic is used by Cicero of Milo who is present in court ; ' this man here '. We might render by ' my client '.

l. 786. **adversi . . . occidunt,** ' they confront and kill ".

l. 787. **reiecta paenula,** ' throwing back his cloak over his shoulder '.

l. 789. **recurrere :** either historic infinitive or dependent on **incipiunt,** l. 791 ; ' ran behind to '.

l. 790. **quod hunc . . . putarent,** ' because they thought that Milo had already been killed '. For **hunc,** see the note on l. 785 above.

The subjunctive is a little unusual. It can hardly be sub-oblique, i.e. in virtual *oratio obliqua,* as is apparasset in l. 779. Perhaps it can be explained as in Roby, section 1746, or in Gildersleeve and Lodge, section 541, note 3.

l. 792. **ex quibus qui,** ' of those who '.

l. 792. **animo fideli . . . et praesenti,** ' of a loyal and resolute spirit ' ; ablative of description or quality.

793. **partim . . . partim,** ' partly . . . partly '. Translate by ' some . . . others '.

l. 794. **cum ad raedam pugnari viderent,** ' when they saw fighting by the carriage '. Note that there are four subjunctive verbs dependent on **cum.**

l. 795. **Milonem occisum (esse)** depends both on **audirent** and **putarent.**

l. 796. et . . . et, ' both . . . and '.

l. 797. non derivandi criminis causa, ' not for the sake of transferring the charge '. Note : (i) causa following its case (genitive). (ii) the gerundive construction, which, in the genitive is an alternative expression to the gerund with a direct object. E.g. Cicero might have written here : non derivandi crimen causa.

l. 798. nec imperante . . . domino, *lit.*, ' their master neither ordering nor knowing nor present ' = ' without the order or knowledge, or presence of their master '. Ablative of attendant circumstances or ablative absolute.

l. 799. quod quisque voluisset, ' what anyone would have wished '. The antecedent of quod is id, l. 797.

Note how Cicero emphasises the fact that Milo's slaves (not Milo) attacked and slew Clodius not only to defend but also to avenge their master.

SECTION 30

Line 801. iudices, ' jurymen '. In this particular trial, there seem to have been 81 jurymen, who were selected by lot from a panel of 360 names, 120 senators, 120 equites and 120 tribuni aerarii. The two latter classes consisted of wealthy but non-noble Romans.

l. 802. est, to be taken both with victa and oppressa.

l. 803. nihil dico quid, ' I say nothing of what '.

l. 804. vos . . . omnes boni ; supply ' gained ' from the preceding consecuta sit. boni, as used by Cicero, meant ' loyal citizens ' who supported the senatorial government. Contrasted with them were mob-leaders like Clodius, revolutionaries and anarchists like the infamous Catiline.

l. 805. nihil sane id prosit Miloni, ' it would in no way benefit Milo '.

l. 806. ut ne se quidem . . . servaret, ' that he could not even save himself but that he saved at the same time (una) his country and you '. Quin, ' but that ', is common after negatives. We might render the quin clause by 'without saving', etc.

l. 808. **nihil habeo quod defendam**, 'I have nothing to plead in his defence'.

l. 809. **sin hoc . . . praescripsit**; in this sentence, there are four subjects, **ratio, necessitas, mos, natura ipsa,** each of which has the same verb praescripsit, the same *direct* object **hoc,** and their own indirect objects **doctis, barbaris, gentibus,** and **feris** respectively.

l. 809. **hoc,** ' this,' i.e. this truth, viz. that violence can lawfully (**iure,** l. 808) be overcome by violence. Cicero elaborates the same idea in the following ut clause.

l. 813. **quin simul iudicetis.** See the note above, l. 806.

l. 814. **omnibus . . . pereundum (esse)**; indirect speech after **iudicetis,** *lit.,* ' that by all who have encountered brigands, there is to be a perishing either by their weapons or by your votes '.

Note : (i) the neuter of the gerundive expressing ' ought ', ' must ', ' should '. This use is confined to the nominative case (accusative also when in indirect speech). The gerundive is used personally with transitive and impersonally (i.e. in the neuter) with intransitive verbs.[1] (ii) **omnibus,** dative of the agent. (iii) **inciderint,** perfect subjunctive, subordinate clause in indirect speech.

We might translate : ' that all who have encountered brigands, must perish, etc.'. Cf. **occidendum Milonem** of l. 747.

A letter to Atticus

Line 816. **numquam** : take this with **legisse.**

l. 816. **ante,** adverb, ' before ', also with **legisse.**

l. 817. **colligere,** ' to surmise ', ' to infer '.

l. 819. **vacui temporis,** partitive genitive, depending on **nihil.**

[1] See also Sallust, Chap. 106, l. 374.

l. 819. **recreandae voculae causa.** See the note on Pro Milone, Section 29, l. 797.

l. 820. **voculae**, ' my poor voice ', which he had strained in the courts.

l. 822. **primum**, ' in the first place '.

l. 822. **illud** is frequently used to point to something which follows. It need not be translated.

l. 822. **Sampsiceramum.** Cicero uses this name of a minor Eastern potentate to refer humorously to the Roman general Pompey. We might then translate by the ' Nabob ' or the ' Pasha ', or the great Panjandrum.

l. 824. **restitui**, present infinitive passive, dependent on cupere. During this year, 59 B.C., Pompey had no official position in the state either as a magistrate or a general. Although he had little aptitude for politics, Pompey seems to have been a vain man, who felt that he always ought to be the most important man in the country : yet, unlike Caesar, he never wished for autocratic power.

l. 825. **nobis.** Translate by the first person singular. The use of the plural seems to carry a suggestion of self-importance. Cf. the use in English of the editorial ' we '.

l. 826. **quam . . . puto**, ' which I think cannot be found at all '.

l. 827. **deinde . . . umquam fuisse.** This sentence is still in indirect speech after te scire volo, l. 822.

l. 828. **nullo adversario**, *lit.*, ' no-one opposing ', ablative absolute, i e. ' although no-one opposes them '.

l. 828. **consenescere**, *lit.*, ' are growing old ' = ' are degenerating ' = ' are losing their power '.

l. 828. **consensionem . . . umquam fuisse**, ' and there never was greater harmony among all either in purpose or in conversation '.

l. 831. **nos . . . intersumus . . . contulimus.** Note the first person plural. Translate by the singular.

l. 832. **ad forensem operam laboremque**, ' to my forensic work and labour ' =' to my work and labours in the courts '.

l. 834. **in multa commemoratione ... versamur,** ' I live in deep remembrance and longing for those things which I have done '.

earum rerum, objective genitive, depends both on com-memoratione and on desiderio.

Cicero could never forget his triumph when as consul in 63 B.C. he crushed a very dangerous conspiracy on the part of Catiline, to overthrow the constitution by a *coup d'état*. By the date of this letter, 59 B.C., Cicero was politically insignificant, and the republican traditions and forms of government which he revered so much, were already threatened by Julius Caesar and flouted by unscrupulous gangsters like Clodius. Cicero's activities as a lawyer—a sphere in which he remained always supreme—constantly remind him of the republic's and his own achievements.

l. 835. βοώπιδος **nostrae consanguineus.** βοῶπις ' great-eyed ', is an epithet which Homer [1] uses in his poems the *Iliad* and the *Odyssey* of the goddess Hera, the wife of Zeus. Thus the phrase in the text means ' the kinsman of our " great-eyed " girl ', i.e. the infamous Clodius who, as we learned in the preceding *Pro Milone*, was killed in a scuffle on the Appian Way with Milo and his retinue. ' The " great-eyed " girl ' is Clodius' sister, Clodia, a Roman beauty, famous for her blazing eyes and her unhappy love affair with the Roman poet Catullus.

l. 836. **non mediocres terrores iacit atque denuntiat,** ' is inspiring and threatening no mean terrors '. Perhaps we could say ' terrible reports ' for **non mediocres terrores.** Clodius is canvassing, or rather using gangster methods in his candidature, for the tribuneship.

l. 837. **Sampsiceramo ... ostentat,** ' he denies (them) to the Nabob (but) parades and displays them to others '.

l. 839. **tantum quantum,** ' as much as '.

[1] Homer, the Greek epic poet, lived and wrote about 800 B.C.

l. 840. **expergiscere . . . ingredere,** second person singular, imperative passive (of deponents).

l. 842. **quod maximum est,** 'what is most important' refers to what follows.

l. 845. **coniunctio,** etc. Supply ' but ' before this sentence. This absence of a conjunction (asyndeton) is typical of Latin, which prefers to obtain contrast by mere apposition of phrases and clauses.

l. 846. **permagni nostra interest,** ' it is of great importance to us '. Note this impersonal use of **interesse,** with the genitive of price (or it may be a locative) and **nostra.** Normally the person to whom it is of importance is in the genitive, but, instead of the genitive of personal pronouns, the ablative singular feminine of the possessive adjective is used. See also Sallust, Ch. III, l. 454.

l. 847. **illo declarato,** ' when he (i.e. Clodius) is declared (elected) '.

l. 848. **cura ut valeas,** ' see to it that you are well ', i.e. ' look after yourself '.

The Friendship of Laelius and Scipio

Line 849. **si . . . negem,** ' should I deny '. In conditional sentences of the ideal type, the supposition is more or less fanciful : the present or perfect (for completed action) subjunctive is used in both protasis and apodosis. The apodosis of this sentence is interrupted by the parenthetic clause **quam id . . . sapientes.**

l. 850. **quam . . . sapientes,** ' wise men (i.e. the philosophers) would see how right I am in doing that '. **viderint,** perfect subjunctive (potential).

l. 851. **tali amico . . . qualis,** ' of such a friend . . . as '.

l. 856. **nihil mali,** ' no harm '. Note the partitive genitive.

l. 857. **si quid,** ' if any '. Note **quis, quid,** ' anyone ', ' anything ', after **si, nisi, num, ne.**

l. 857. **Suis . . . amantis est.** The subject of **est** is **suis** incommodis graviter angi, ' to be greatly distressed at one's own misfortunes '. amantis, ' (the characteristic) of one who loves ' ; this participle has amicum and se ipsum as direct objects.

l. 859. cum illo ... praeclare. Note the phrase agi praeclare, ' to go wonderfully well '.

l. 860. immortalitem, ' freedom from death '.

l. 863. de eo iam puero, ' of him in his childhood '.

l. 865. factus est consul bis, i.e. first in 147 B.C., before he was of legal age (ante tempus), when in his thirty-eighth year he was a candidate for the aedileship, and again in 134 B.C.

l. 866. ante tempus ... suo tempore, ' before the (proper) time ' ... ' at the right time '.

l. 867. qui ... delevit. Translate eversis by a present participle, ' by overthrowing ', and take huic imperio with inimicissimis. The two cities which Scipio destroyed were Carthage (146 B.C.) and Numantia in Central Spain (133 B.C.)

l. 870. in matrem, ' towards his mother '. Similarly in sorores etc.

l. 873. maerore funeris, ' by the sorrow shown at his funeral '.

l. 873. quid, ' how '.

l. 874. potuisset, ' would have been able '. This sub-junctive can be explained as conditional (unreal in past time) : the apodosis can easily be supplied from accessio, e.g. ' if he had lived any longer '.

l. 876. Catonem. This is the Elder Cato (234-149 B.C.), distinguished for his military ability, integrity, and un-bending severity. He is the great-grandfather of the Cato whom Cicero mentions in his speech (Pro Milone, l. 757).

l. 876. ante quam mortuus est. Note the indicative mood, which shows that the sentence is an addition by Laelius and not part of what he remembered.

l. 877. eam viriditatem, ' that freshness '.

l. 879. **vel fortuna, vel gloria,** ablative case, to be taken with accedere. The latter is frequently used as the passive of addo, ' to be added '.

l. 882. **difficile dictu,** ' difficult to speak '. Note that the ablative of the supine is used chiefly with adjectives (ablative of respect).

l. 882. **quid homines suspicentur,** viz. that he was murdered shortly after his return from Spain (129 B.C.).

l. 883. **ex multis diebus . . . viderit,** ' of the many glorious and joyful days which he saw in the course of his life '. Note the position of the superlative adjectives, which are inside the relative clause and in agreement with the relative pronoun, though in sense they belong to the antecedent, multis diebus.

l. 885. **senatu dimisso,** ' on the adjournment of the senate '.

l. 886. **domum reductus . . . Latinis.** Scipio was escorted home by ' allies ' and ' Latins ', because he had that day defended their interest in the public land against the ' commission of three men ' (Triumvirs) who had been appointed by the agrarian law of Tiberius Gracchus to reclaim and distribute in small holdings large tracts of public land.

Allies were united to Rome by treaties, Latins (i.e. those of the Latin status) were incorporated in the Roman commonwealth and possessed the ' private rights ' of citizenship (**ius commercii, ius conubii,**[1] but not the ' public rights ' (**ius suffragii, ius honorum** [2]).

[1] Right to conduct private suits in the Roman court, and contract a legal marriage.

[2] Right to vote and to hold office.

VOCABULARY

(In the following vocabulary only irregular verbs are given their principal parts in full. Otherwise the figures (1), (2), (3), (4), following a verb denote that it is a regular example of that conjugation. No conjugation number is given in the case of -io verbs like capio.)

A

a *or* **ab**, *prep. with abl.*, by, from ; **a cornu**, on the flank.

abdo, -didi, -ditum (3), hide, conceal.

abeo, -ire, -ii, -itum, depart, leave.

abhorreo, -ui (2), be averse from, disinclined to.

abripio, -ere, -ripui, -reptum, carry off.

absolvo, -solvi, -solutum, acquit.

absterreo (2), frighten off *or* away.

absum, -esse, **abfui**, be absent, distant.

ac, and, and moreover.

accedo, -cessi, -cessum (3), approach; accede to; be added.

accelero (1), hasten, quicken.

accendo, -ndi, -nsum (3), light.

acceptus, -a, -um, acceptable, welcome.

accerso, -ivi, -itum (3), send for, invite.

accessio, -ionis, *f.*, addition.

accido, -cidi (3), happen.

accingo, -nxi, -nctum (3), gird on ; *in pass.*, make oneself ready for (*Livy, Scaevola*).

accio (4), send for, invite.

accipio, -ere, -cepi, -ceptum, receive ; hear (*of news*).

accuso (1), accuse.

acer, -cris, -cre, vigorous, keen, spirited.

acies, -ei, *f.*, line (*of battle*).

ad, *prep. with acc.*, to, towards ; at, near; for, for the purpose of

adcurro, -curri, -cursum (3), run up to.

addo, -didi, -ditum (3), add.

adduco, -duxi, -ductum (3), bring word.

adeo, -ire, -ii, -itum, go to, approach.

adeo, *adv.*, so, to such an extent.

adfero, -ferre, **attuli**, **adlatum**, bring news.

adfinitas, -tatis, *f.*, relationship.

adfirmo (1), strengthen.

adhibeo (2), use, employ ; summon.

adhortatio, -ionis, *f.*, exhortation, urging.

adhuc, *adv.*, as yet.

adipiscor, -eptus (3), obtain, acquire, get.

aditus, -us, *m.*, approach, entrance, access.

adiuvo, -iuvi, -iutum (1), help, support ; contribute.

administro (1), manage, arrange.

adno (1), swim to.

adorior, -ortus (4), attack.

adprobo (1), approve (of).

adsum, -esse, -fui, be present, be at hand, appear.

adulescens, -entis, m., young man.

adulescentia, -ae, f., youth, immaturity.

advenio, -veni, -ventum (4), arrive.

advento (1), approach.

adventus, -us, m., approach, coming ; arrival.

adversarius, -i, m., opponent, enemy.

adversum, prep. with acc., against.

adversus = adversum.

adversus, -a, -um, facing, in front.

advolo (1), fly ; swoop down.

aedes, -is, f., house.

aeger, -gra, -grum, sick.

Aeolis, -idis, f., district of Asia Minor, stretching from the Dardanelles southwards along the coast.

aequus, -a, -um, level ; fair, favourable ; aequo animo, patiently, calmly, resignedly.

aestimo (1), estimate, assess.

Africa, -ae, f., Africa.

ager, agri, m., field, land.

aggredior, -i, aggressus, attack.

agito (1), set in motion ; meditate, ponder ; resolve on.

agmen, -inis, n., column.

ago, egi, actum (3) do, act ; negotiate (Caesar) ; multa agere, to be busy ; familiariter agere, be on friendly terms.

agrestis, -e, brutish, rude.

alacritas, -tatis, f., glee, joy.

alieno (1), estrange ; sever.

alienus, -a, -um, belonging to another, another ; out of place (Nepos).

aliquamdiu, adv., for some time.

aliquando, adv., at last, at length.

aliquantus, -a, -um, considerable.

aliqui, -qua, -quod, adj., some, any.

aliquis, -qua, -quid, pronoun, some-one, some-thing ; anyone, anything.

aliter, adv., otherwise.

alius, -a, -ud, other, another ; alii . . . alii, some . . . others.

alo, alui, altum (3), maintain, feed.

altaria, -ium, n. pl., altar.

alter, -era, -erum, another (of two), a second.

altitudo, -inis, f., height.

altus, -a, -um, high, lofty.

ambages, -is, f. (a roundabout way) ; evasion, riddle (Livy, Scaevola).

ambo, -ae, -o, both.

ambulo (1), walk.

amicitia, -ae, f., friendship ; alliance.

amicus, -i, m., friend ; as adj., friendly.

amitto, -misi, -missum (3), lose.

amo (1), like, love.

amor, -oris, m., love, affection.

amoveo, -movi, -motum (2), move from.

amplius, *adv.,* more than.

amplus, -a, -um, great (*of number*).

an, *interrog. particle,* or.

ancilla, -ae, *f.,* maid.

ango, anxi (3), pain, grieve, torment.

animadverto, -ti, -sum (3), observe, notice.

animus, -i, *m.,* mind, feeling, courage, spirit.

Anio, -enis, *m.,* the Anio, a river, tributary of the Tiber.

annus, -i, *m.,* year.

ante, *prep. with acc.,* before; outside (*Caesar*); *adv.,* earlier, before.

antea, *adv.,* before.

antequam, *conj.,* before.

aperio, -erui, -ertum (4), disclose, reveal.

aperte, *adv.,* openly.

apertus, -a, -um, open, exposed.

appareo (2), come in sight, appear.

appello (1), call, call upon.

appello, -puli, -pulsum (3), bring; (*of ships*), put in, bring to land.

Appenninus, -i, *m.,* the Apennines.

appropinquo (1), approach, come near.

aptus, -a, -um, fitted.

apud, *prep. with acc.,* with, among; in; in the hands of (*Sallust*).

aqua, -ae, *f.,* water.

arbitratus, -us, *m.,* mediation.

arbitror (1), think, consider.

arbor, -oris, *f.,* tree.

arma, -orum, *n. pl.,* arms, weapons.

armatus, -a, ·um, armed.

Artaphernes, -is, *m.,* Artaphernes, Persian satrap in command of the Persian fleet.

arx, arcis, *f.,* citadel.

Asia, -ae, *f.,* Asia; Asia Minor.

Aspar, -aris, *m.,* Aspar, a Numidian, envoy of Jugurtha to Bocchus.

at, but.

Athenae, -arum, *f. pl.,* Athens.

Atheniensis, -is, *m.,* an Athenian; *as adj.,* Athenian.

atque, and, and moreover; *after* totidem, =as.

Attica, -ae, *f.,* Attica.

attineo, -tinui, -tentum (2), detain, delay.

Attius, -i, *m.,* Attius.

attonitus, -a, -um, stunned, thunderstruck.

auctor, -oris, *m.,* promoter (*Cicero*); informant (*Caesar*); principal (*Nepos*).

auctoritas, -tatis, *f.,* influence, authority.

audacia, -ae, *f.,* daring, boldness; insolence (*Cicero*).

audax, -acis, daring, bold.

audeo, ausus sum (2), dare, venture.

audio (4), hear, listen to.

augeo, auxi, auctum (2), increase.

aufero, -ferre, abstuli, ablatum, take away.

augustus, -a, -um, majestic, magnificent.

auris, -is, *f.,* ear.

aut, or; **aut . . . aut,** either . . . or.

autem, but, however; (*in narrative*), now.

auxilium, -i, *n.*, help, support; *in pl.*, auxiliaries, reinforcements.

averto, -ti, -sum (3), turn aside; aversos proterere, to ride down.

avidus, -a, -um, eager.

B

Bagradas, -ae, the River Bagradas, near Utica (N. Africa).

Baleares, -ium, *m.*, Balearic slingers.

barba, -ae, *f.*, beard.

barbarus, -a, -um, foreign, barbarian; uncivilised (*Cicero*); *as noun*, barbarian.

bellum, -i, *n.*, war.

bene, *adv.*, well, successfully.

beneficium, -i, *n.*, kindness, service.

benigne, *adv.*, affably, kindly.

bis, *adv.*, twice.

Bocchus, -i, *m.*, Bocchus.

bonitas, -tatis, *f.*, goodness, kindness; honesty (*Nepos*).

bonus, -a, -um, good; high (*of hopes*); boni, -orum, loyal citizens.

brevitas, -tatis, *f.*, brevity.

breviter, *adv.*, briefly.

C

C., abbreviation for Gaius.

cado, cecidi, casum (3), fall.

caedes, -is, *f.*, murder, slaughter.

caedo, cecidi, caesum (3), kill, slay.

Caesar, C. Iulius, Julius Caesar.

calceus, -i, *m.*, shoe.

calliditas, -tatis, *f.*, cunning.

campus, -i, *m.*, plain.

cantus, -us, *m.*, song.

capio, -ere, cepi, captum, seize, capture, occupy; contain (*Livy, Gauls*).

Capitolium, -i, *n.*, the Capitol (*in Rome*).

captivus, -i, *m.*, prisoner.

caput, -itis, *n.*, head; life; leader.

careo, (2) *with abl.*, be without, be free from.

caritas, -tatis, *f.*, dearness, high price.

carus, -a, -um, dear.

castra, -orum, *n. pl.*, camp.

casus, -us, *m.*, chance.

Cato, -onis, Marcus Cato, the elder (234–149 B.C.).

Cato, -onis, Marcus Cato, the younger (95–46 B.C.), contemporary of Cicero and opponent of Caesar.

causa, -ae, *f.*, reason, cause, case; *abl.*, causā, *as prep.*, for the sake of.

caveo, cavi, cautum (2), be on one's guard, guard against.

cedo, cessi, cessum (3), yield, give ground, retire, withdraw.

celeber, -bris, -bre, distinguished.

celer, -eris, -ere, quick, swift, rapid.

celeritas, -tatis, *f.*, speed, swiftness; suddenness (*Cicero*).

celeriter, *adv.*, quickly, swiftly.

ceno (1), have supper; cenatus, having supped, after supper.

centum, a hundred.

centurio, -ionis, *m.*, centurion.

cerno, crevi, cretum (3), perceive, see.

certe, *adv.*, certainly.

certo, *adv.*, certainly, surely.

certus, -a, -um, certain, sure, reliable.

ceterum, but, however.

ceterus, -a, -um, the other, the remaining.

Chersonesus, -i, *f.*, the Chersonese (*peninsula west of the Dardanelles*).

circa, *prep. with acc.*, around.

circiter, *prep. with acc.*, about; *as adv.*, about.

circueo, -ire, -ii, -itum, surround, work round.

circum, *prep. with acc.*, round, around, about.

circumaro (1), plough around.

circumdo, -dedi, -datum (1), surround, hem in; place *or* set around (*Livy, Scaevola*).

circumeo, -ire, -ii, -itum, go round, visit.

circumfero, -ferre, -tuli, -latum, cast around.

circummunio (4), encircle.

circumsisto, -stiti, (3), stand around.

circumspecto (1), look around.

circumvenio, -veni, -ventum (4), envelop, surround, cut off.

citatus, -a, -um, at the double.

civis, -is, *c.*, citizen, fellow-citizen.

civitas, -tatis, *f.*, state, community.

clam, *adv.*, secretly, unobserved.

clamor, -oris, *m.*, shout, cry.

clarus, -a, -um, distinguished, brilliant.

classiarius, -i, *m.*, marine.

classis, -is, *f.*, fleet.

claudo, -si, -sum (3), shut; surround, encompass.

Clodius, -i, *m.*, Clodius.

Cn. = Gnaeus.

coacervo (1), heap up, collect together.

Cocles, -itis, *m.* (=one-eyed), cognomen of Horatius.

coepi, -isse, coeptus sum, began.

cogito (1), think.

cognatio, -ionis, *f.*, kinship.

cognosco, -novi, -nitum (3), learn, discover, ascertain; examine (*a case*).

cogo, coegi, coactum (3), compel, collect.

cohors, -hortis, *f.*, cohort.

cohortatio, -ionis, *f.*, encouragement, exhortation.

cohortor (1), urge.

coicio, -ere, -ieci, -iectum, cast, hurl, throw.

collega, -ae, *m.*, colleague.

colligo, -legi, -lectum (3), infer.

Collinus, -a, -um, Colline (*pertaining to north-eastern hills of Rome*).

collis, -is, *m.*, hill.

colloco (1), post, station.

colloquium, -i, *n.*, parley, conference.

colo, colui, cultum (3), revere, reverence, worship.

comes, -itis, *m.*, companion.

comitatus, -us, *m.*, train, retinue.

comitium, -i, *n.*, comitium, an open space to the N.E. of the Forum in Rome.

comitia, -orum, *n. pl.*, elections.

commeatus, -us, *m.*, supplies, provisions.

commemoratio, -ionis, *f.*, remembrance.

commemoro (1), relate, report.

commendo (1), recommend, entrust.

comminus, *adv.*, at close quarters, hand to hand.

committo, -misi, -missum (3), entrust; committere proelium, join battle.

commoror (1), wait.

commoveo, -movi, -motum (2), move strongly; arouse, stir.

communis, -e, common, general, public.

communitas, -tatis, *f.*, sociability.

commuto (1), change entirely

comparo (1), get ready, prepare.

comperio, -perui, -pertum (4), find; learn.

comperior, *dep.*, find, ascertain.

competitor, -oris, *m.*, rival, opponent.

compleo, -plevi, -pletum (2), fill; throng (*Caesar*); make up (*Nepos*).

comploro (1), bewail, mourn (*transitive*).

compono, -posui, -positum (3), arrange, prepare.

comprehendo, -ndi, -nsum (3), seize.

concedo, -cessi, -cessum (3), withdraw.

concursatio, -ionis, *f.*, a running about, a going to and fro.

concursus, -us, *m.*, crowd, throng.

condicio, -ionis, *f.*, agreement; *pl.*, terms.

confero, -ferre, -tuli, collatum, collect; compare (*Caesar*); se conferre, betake oneself to; devote oneself to (*Cicero*).

confertus, -a, -um, massed together; thickest.

conficio, -ere, -feci, -fectum, finish, complete; exhaust.

confido, -fisus sum (3), trust; trust in, rely on (*with dat. of person, or abl. of thing*).

confirmo (1), strengthen; affirm, confirm; vow.

confligo, -flixi, -flictum (3), fight.

congero, -gessi, gestum (3), collect.

conglobo (1) (*especially in pass.*), gather together (*intransitive*).

congredior, -i, -gressus, meet.

conicio, *see* coicio.

coniunctio, -ionis, *f.*, intimacy.

coniungo, -iunxi, -iunctum (3), join, ally.

coniunx, coniugis, *f.*, wife.

coniuro (1), form a conspiracy, plot.

conor (1), try, endeavour.

consanguineus, -i, *m.*, kinsman.

conscendo, -ndi, -nsum (3), embark.

conscius, -a, -um, knowing, privy.

conscribo, -psi, -ptum (3), enlist, enrol.

conscripti, -orum, *m. pl.*, the elected (fathers), =senators.

consenesco, -senui (3), (grow old); lose power.

consensio, -ionis, *f.*, agreement, harmony.

consensus, -us, *m.*, agreement.

consequor, -secutus (3), obtain, gain.

consido, -sedi, -sessum (3), take up a position, encamp.

consilium, -i, *n.*, plan, purpose, intention ; arrangement.

consisto, -stiti, -stitum (3), halt, take a position.

consolor (1), console, comfort.

conspectus, -us, *m.*, sight, presence.

conspicio, -ere, -spexi, -spectum, catch sight of, perceive, see.

conspicor (1), catch sight of.

constituo, -ui, -utum (3), draw up ; determine, decide, resolve ; erect (*mantlets, etc.*)

consto, -stiti, -statum (1) consist.

consuesco, -suevi, suetum (3), am accustomed.

consuetudo, -inis, *f.*, habit, custom.

consul, -is, *m.*, consul.

consularis, -e, consular (*one who has held office as consul*).

consulatus, -us, *m.*, consulship.

consulo, -ului, -ultum (3), consult (*with acc.*); take thought; have regard to, consult interests of (*with dat.*)

consulto, *adv.*, purposely.

contendo, -di, -tum (3), hasten ; make all speed.

contentio, -ionis, *f.*, struggle (*Caesar*) ; controversy.

contentus, -a, -um, contented, satisfied.

conterritus, -a, -um, terrified.

continens, -ntis, following, next, consequent upon.

continens, -ntis, *m.*, mainland.

continuo, *adv.*, at once, forthwith.

contio, -ionis, *f.*, meeting.

contra, *prep. with acc.*, against.

controversia, -ae, *f.*, quarrel, dispute.

convalesco, -valui (3), gain strength.

convenio, -veni, -ventum (4), come together, meet, assemble (*Caesar*) ; agree ; agree upon ; conclude (*of peace*).

conventus, -us, *m.*, *see note on* Caesar, Chap. 36, l. 159.

convoco (1), call together, assemble.

copia, -ae, *f.*, plenty, abundance ; *in pl.*, forces.

coram, *prep. with abl.*, in the presence of.

Cornelianus, -a, -um, Cornelian.

corpus, -oris, *n.*, body ; person (*Livy, Horatius*).

corrumpo, -rupi, -ruptum (3), corrupt.

creber, -bra, -brum, numerous, frequent.

crebro, *adv.*, frequently, repeatedly.

credibilis, -e, believable.

credo, credidi, creditum (3), believe, have confidence in (+ *dat.*) ; entrust (+ *dat.*).

creo (1), elect.

crimen, -inis, *n.*, charge, accusation.

cruentus, -a, -um, bloodstained.

cultus, -us (4), worship.

cum, *conjunction*, when, since ; cum ... tum, not only ... but also ; both ... and.

cum, *prep. with abl.*, with.

cumulus, -i, *m.*, mound, heap.

cuncti, -ae, -a, all.

cunctor (1), hesitate.

cupiditas, -tatis, *f.*, desire, eagerness.

cupio, -ere, cupivi, cupitum, desire, wish.

curator, -oris, *m.*, delegate.

Curio, -ionis, *m.*, Curio.

curo (1), take care of ; see to.

curro, cucurri, cursum (3), run.

cursor, -oris, *m.*, courier.

custodia, -ae, *f.*, protection.

custos, -odis, *m.*, picket, sentry ; guardian (*Nepos*).

curulis, -e, curule.

D

Dabar, -aris, *m.*, Dabar, a Numidian, friend of Bocchus.

damnatio, -ionis, *f.*, conviction, condemnation.

Darius, -i, *m.*, Darius, king of the Persians.

Datis, -is, *m.*, Datis, satrap of Darius.

de, *prep. with abl.*, from, down from ; concerning, about, of.

debeo (2), owe.

debilis, -e, weak, disabled.

decem, ten.

decemplex, -icis, ten times as great.

decerno, -crevi, -cretum (3), decide ; (decide by combat) =fight ; appoint, fix, decree.

decessus, -us, *m.*, death, decease.

decido, -cidi (3), fall, drop.

decimus, -a, -um, tenth.

declaro (1), declare (*elected to office*).

decurro, -curri, -cursum (3), run *or* rush down.

decus, -oris, *n.*, glory, honour, renown.

deditio, -ionis, *f.*, surrender.

dedo, -didi, -ditum (3), surrender.

deduco, -duxi, -ductum (3), lead down ; take (*Sallust*) ; land (*of troops, Nepos*).

defendo, -fendi, -fensum (3), defend, protect.

defensio, -ionis, *f.*, defence.

defero, -ferre, -tuli, -latum, report (*of news*).

defessus, -a, -um, weary, exhausted, fatigued.

deficio, -ficere, -feci, -fectum, fail, be lacking, run short.

defigo, -fixi, -fixum (3), stupefy, astound.

dein, *adv.*, then, next.

deinde, *adv.*, then, next.

deleo, -evi, -etum (2), destroy.

deligo, -legi, -lectum (3), choose.

Demetrius, -i, *m.*, Demetrius of Phalerus (Phalareus).

demigro (1), depart.

demonstro (1), explain, mention.

demum, *adv.*, at last, in fact indeed.

denique, *adv.*, only, not until.

denuntio (1), threaten.

depingo, -pinxi, -pictum (3), depict, paint.

deploro (1), give up for lost, abandon.

depopulor (1), plunder, pillage, raid.

deprendo (deprehendo), -di, -sum (3), catch, seize, capture.

derivo (1), turn aside, transfer.

deprimo, -pressi, -pressum (3), sink.

desero, -serui, -sertum (3), abandon, desert.

desiderium, -i, n., longing (for).

desidero (1), miss, need.

desilio, -silui, -sultum (4), leap down.

desperatio, -ionis, f., despair.

despero (1), despair.

destino (1), devote, destine.

destituo, -ui, -utum (3), place or set down.

desum, -esse, -fui, be lacking.

deterreo (2), deter.

detrudo, -si, -sum (3), dislodge, dispossess.

deus, -i, n. pl. di, gen. pl. deum, dat. abl. pl. dis, god.

dexter, -ra, -rum, or -tera, -terum, right; **dextra**, -ae, f., the right hand.

dico, **dixi**, **dictum** (3), say, tell.

dictator, -oris, m., dictator.

dictito (1), maintain.

dicto (1), dictate.

dies, -ei, f., day; in dies, from day to day, daily; dies insequens, the following day.

differo, -ferre, distuli, dilatum, postpone.

difficilis, -e, difficult.

dignitas, -tatis, f., rank, position.

dignus, -a, -um (+ abl)., worthy.

digredior, -i, -gressus, go away, depart.

dilabor, -lapsus (3), flee, escape, scatter.

dilacero (1), tear to pieces.

dilectus, -us, m., levy.

dimico (1), struggle.

dimitto, -misi, -missum (3), let go, release; let slip; adjourn (the senate).

diripio, -ere, -ripui, -reptum, plunder.

discedo, -cessi, -cessum (3), go away, leave, depart; with **ab**, abandon, give up, desert.

discrimen, -inis, n., peril, risk, danger.

dispersus, -a, -um, scattered, dispersed.

dissero, -serui, -sertum (3), discuss.

dissipo (1), scatter, disperse.

diu, adv., for a long time.

dissonus, -a, -um, discordant.

distineo, -tinui, -tentum (2), occupy, engage.

diuturnitas, -tatis, f., long duration.

do, **dedi**, **datum** (1), give.

doceo, -ui, -ctum (2), point out.

doctus, -i, m., learned man.

doleo (2), regret.

dolor, -oris, m., resentment, anger.

dolus, -i, m., fraud, deceit, treachery.

dominatio, -ionis, f., tyranny.

dominus, -i, m., master.

Domitius, -i, m., Domitius.

domus, -us, f., home, house; domi, loc., at home.

dormio (4), sleep, be asleep.

dubito (1), doubt.

dubius, -a, -um, uncertain, wavering.

ducenti, -ae, -a, two hundred.

duco, -xi, -ctum (3), lead; prolong (*Caesar*).

dum, *conj.*, while, until.

dumtaxat, *adv.*, only, merely.

duo, -ae, -o, two.

dux, -cis, guide.

E

e, *see* **ex.**

eburneus, -a, -um, ivory.

edoceo, -cui, -ctum (2), instruct, inform.

educo, -xi, -ctum (3), lead out; draw (*of a sword*).

efficio, -ere, -feci, -fectum, render, produce.

effugio, -ere, -fugi, escape, avoid.

effuse, *adv.*, far and wide.

effusus, -a, -um, *perf. part. pass. of* effundo, straggling, disorderly, scattered; profuse, unreserved (*Nepos*).

egeo (2), *with abl.*, want, need.

ego, 1*st person pron.*, I.

egomet, 1*st person pron.*, I myself.

egredior, -i, egressus, go out, march out, leave.

elatus, -a, -um, elated, puffed up.

elephantus, -i, *m.*, elephant.

eligo, -legi, -lectum (3), pick out, choose.

emineo (2), stand out, be conspicuous.

en, *interjection*, lo! behold!

enim, *conj.*, for.

eo, ire, ii *or* **ivi, itum,** go.

eo, *adv.*, to that place, thither, there.

eo magis, the more so.

eodem, *adv.*, to the same place.

epistula, -ae, *f.*, letter.

eques, -itis, *m.*, cavalry-man, trooper; *in pl.*, cavalry.

equitatus, -us, *m.*, cavalry.

equus, -i, *m.*, horse.

Eretria, -ae, *f.*, Eretria (*town on the island of Euboea off the east coast of Attica*).

erga, *prep. with acc.*, towards (*in relations other than motion*).

ergo, *adv.*, therefore.

eripio, -ere, -ripui, -reptum, take away.

error, -oris, *m.*, mistake, error.

et, and; **et . . . et,** both . . . and.

etenim, *conj.*, for.

etiam, and also, also, too, even.

etiamnunc, even now.

etsi, although, though.

Etruria, -ae, *f.*, Etruria (*district north of Rome*).

Etrusci, -orum, *m. pl.*, the Etruscans (*natives of Etruria*).

Euboea, -ae, *f.*, Euboea (*island off the east coast of Attica*).

Europa, -ae, *f.*, Europe.

everto, -si, -sum (3), overthrow.

ex *or* **e,** *prep. with abl.*, out of, from; in consequence of; in accordance with.

exanimo (1), terrify, agitate.

excedo, -cessi, -cessum (3), go away, retire, leave; **excedere e vita,** to die.

excipio, -ere, -cepi, -ceptum, catch; receive, sustain; befall.

excludo, -di, -sum (3), cut off.

excubo, -bui, -bitum (1), keep watch.

exeo, -ire, -ii, -itum, go out.

exercitus, -us, *m.*, army.

exhaurio, -hausi, -haustum (4), pillage.

exiguus, -a, -um, small.

existimo (1), think, consider.

exitium, -i, *n.*, destruction.

expedio (4), prepare, set in order ; be expedient (*Nepos*).

expeditus, -a, -um, unencumbered; light-armed.

expello, -puli, -pulsum (3), drive out, expel.

expergiscor, -rectus (3), awake.

experior, expertus (4), learn *or* know by experience ; test, try.

explorator, -oris, *m.*, scout.

exploro (1), reconnoitre.

expono, -posui, -positum (3), relate, explain.

expromo, -prompsi, -promptum (3), disclose, declare.

expugno (1), attack, storm.

exquiro, -sivi, -situm (3) inquire.

exspecto (1), wait for, await.

exstinguo, -nxi, -nctum (3), destroy, put an end to.

exsto (1), stand out, show.

extimesco, -mui (3), fear greatly, dread.

F

facile, *adv.*, easily ; *comp.*, facilius ; *superl.*, facillime.

facilis, -e, easy, light ; easy, affable (*Cicero*).

facinus, -oris, *n.*, deed ; crime (*Cicero*).

facio, -ere, feci, factum, do, make, perform.

facta, -orum, *n. pl.*, deeds.

fama, -ae, *f.*, fame, renown.

familiariter, *adv.*, on friendly terms.

fas, *n.*, *indecl.*, proper, right, lawful.

fatigo (1), importune.

fatum, -i, *n.*, fate, destiny.

Favonius, -i, *m.*, Marcus Favonius (*Roman noble and senator*).

Februarius, -a, -um, of February.

fera, -ae, *f.*, wild-beast.

fere, *adv.*, nearly, almost.

fero, ferre, tuli, latum, carry, bear, bring ; endure, tolerate ; win (*Livy, Scaevola*).

ferox, -ocis, spirited.

ferrum, -i, *n.*, sword.

fessus, -a, -um, weary, tired.

fidelis, -e, faithful.

fides, -ei, *f.*, belief, care, honour (*Caesar*) ; conscience, credence (*Livy, Horatius*) ; faith, good faith (*Cicero*).

fiducia, -ae, *f.*, confidence.

fidus, -a, -um, faithful, loyal.

filius, -i, *m.*, son.

finis, -is, *m.*, end ; *in pl.*, borders, territory.

finitimus, -a, -um, neighbouring ; frontier (*as adj., Caesar*).

fio, fieri, factus, am done, am made, happen, take place.

flagro (1), burn.

flamen, -inis, *m.*, priest, flamen.

flamma, -ae, *f.*, flame.

fletus, -us, *m.*, weeping.

flumen, -inis, *n.*, river.

foculum, -i, *n.*, brazier.

foedus, -eris, *n.*, treaty.

fore, *fut. infin. of* sum.

forensis, -e, forensic, of the bar (*legal*).

foret, = esset.

fortasse, *adv.*, perhaps.

forte, *adv.*, by chance.

fortis, -e, brave.

fortuna, -ae, fortune, fate.

forum, -i, *n.*, the forum.

fragor, -oris, *m.*, crash.

frater, -tris, *m.*, brother.

fraus, fraudis, *f.*, deceit, treachery.

fretus, -a, -um, relying on (+ *abl.*).

frumentum, -i, *n.*, corn, grain.

frustra, *adv.*, in vain, uselessly.

fuga, -ae, *f.*, escape, flight, rout.

fugio, -ere, fugi, fugitum, flee.

funditor, -oris, *m.*, slinger.

fundo, -ere, fudi, fusum (3), rout.

fundus, -i, *m.*, estate, homestead.

funus, -eris, *n.*, funeral.

furo (3), be violent *or* mad; rage.

furor, -oris, *m.*, frenzy, mad inspiration.

futurus, -a, -um (*fut. part. of* sum), future.

G

Gallus, -a, -um, Gallic; *as noun*, a Gaul.

genus, -eris, *n.*, kind; class (*Caesar*); rank (*Nepos*); birth (*Livy, Horatius*).

gens, -tis, *f.*, nation; *in pl.*, mankind.

gero, gessi, gestum (3). wage, do. conduct; hold (*of office*); rem gerere, to fight; bear, cherish (*of feelings*); *in passive*, happen.

gladius, -i, *m*, sword.

gloria, -ae, *f.*, glory, fame, renown.

gloriosus, -a, -um, glorious.

gradus, -us, *m.*, step, gait; stage, grade (*Cicero*); rank (*Cicero, Scipio*).

Graecia, -ae, *f.*, Greece.

Graecus, -a, -um, Greek.

grassor (1), advance, make an attack.

gratia, -ae, *f.*, favour, gratitude, kindness; gratiam referre, show gratitude, return thanks.

gratus, -a, -um, welcome, pleasing.

gravis, -e, burdensome.

graviter, *adv.*, seriously, grievously.

guberno (1), guide, control, manage.

H

habeo (2), have, hold (*a meeting*); keep; consider (*Nepos*).

habito (1). live (in). dwell.

habitus, -us, *m.*. bearing.

haereo, -si, -sum (2). stick.

haesito(1), hesitate, be irresolute.

haud, *adv.*, not.

hemerodromus, *pl.*, -dromoe (*one who runs all day*), a courier.

Herminius, -i, *m.*, Titus Herminius.

hic, haec, hoc, this; he, she, it, they; my client (*Cicero*).

hinc, *adv.*, hence, from here.

Hispania, -ae, *f.*, Spain.

Hispanus, -a, -um, Spanish.

Hister, -tri, *m.*, the Hister (*lower part of the Danube*).

Histiaeus, -i, *m.*, Histiaeus.

homo, -inis, *c.*, human, man; fellow (*Cicero*).

honos *or* honor, -oris, *m.*, honour, rank, office.

hora, -ae, *f.*, hour.

Horatius, -i, *m.*, Horatius.

hortor (1), encourage, urge, exhort.

hostilis, -e, hostile, of the enemy.

huc, *adv.*, hither, to this place; here.

humanitas, -tatis, *f.*, refinement.

humanus, -a, -um, human.

humilis, -e, humble.

I

iacio, -ere, ieci, iactum, throw, hurl.

iacto (1), utter.

iactura, -ae, *f.*, loss.

iam, *adv.*, now, already.

Ianiculum, -i, *n.*, Janiculum (*a hill near Rome, west of the Tiber*).

ibi, *adv.*, there.

ibidem, *adv.*, just there, on the spot.

idem, eadem, idem, the same.

identidem, *adv.*, again and again; repeatedly.

idoneus, -a, -um, suitable, fit.

igitur, therefore, accordingly, so.

ignarus, -a, -um, ignorant, not knowing.

ignavia, -ae, *f.*, fault.

ignis, -is, *m.*, fire.

ignoro (1), not know.

ignotus, -a, -um, unknown.

ilico, *adv.*, immediately, instantly.

ille, illa, illud, that; he, she, it, they.

imago, -inis, *f.*, picture.

imbellis, -e, unwarlike, non-combatant.

immemor, -oris, unmindful.

immineo (2), threaten (*with dat.*)

imminuo, -minui, -minutum (3), lessen, diminish.

immortalitas, -tatis, *f.*, immortality.

immuto (1), change.

impedimentum, -i, *n.*, hindrance; *in pl.*, luggage (*Cicero*).

impedio (4), hinder, obstruct.

impeditus, -a, -um, encumbered.

impello, -puli, -pulsum (3), drive, urge on.

imperator, -oris, *m.*, general.

imperium, -i, *n.*, power, military command; empire (*Cicero*).

impero (1), order, command; demand (*Sallust*).

impertio (4), communicate, impart.

impetus, -us, *m.*, charge, attack.

impleo, -plevi, -pletum, fill up.

improbus, -a, -um, wicked.

improviso, de, unexpectedly.

imprudens, -ntis, unsuspecting, off one's guard, unprepared.

in, *prep. with acc.*, to, into, towards; *prep. with abl.*, in, on.

incendium, -i, *n.*, fire.

incendo, -di, -nsum (3), burn.

incertus, -a, -um, uncertain.

incido, -cidi (3), fall into the hands of; encounter.

incipio, -ere, -cepi, -ceptum, begin.

incito (1), excite, urge.

incolo, -colui (3), inhabit, dwell in.

incolumis, -e, safe, unhurt.

incommodum, -i, *n.*, misfortune, trouble.

incredibilis, -e, incredible.

increpo, -ui, itum (1), upbraid, taunt.

inde, *adv.*, thence, from there; then.

indico (1), show.

indico, -xi, -ctum (3), declare (*war*).

indignitas, -tatis, *f.*, insult.

indignus, -a, -um, intolerable.

indigus, -a, -um, in want.

ineo, -ire, -ivi *or* -ii, -itum, enter upon; begin.

inermus, -a, -um, unarmed.

infectus, -a, -um, unaccomplished.

infensus, -a, -um, hostile; enraged (*Livy, Scaevola*).

inferi, -orum, *m. pl.*, the dead, those below.

infero, -ferre, -tuli, illatum, bring in, carry (*Caesar*); cause; bellum inferre, to make war on; signa inferre, to advance, attack.

infestus, -a, -um, hostile.

inflatus, -a, -um, exaggerated.

ingens, -ntis, huge, vast.

ingredior, -i, -gressus, enter upon, enter; proceed (*Cicero*).

inicio, -ere, -ieci, -iectum, thrust in.

inimicus, -i, *m.*, enemy.

iniussu (*abl. of* iniussus), without command.

initium, -i, *n.*, beginning.

iniuria, -ae, *f.*, wrong; attack.

innoxius, -a, -um, not guilty, innocent.

inopia, -ae, *f.*, lack, want, scarcity.

inopinans, -ntis, unsuspecting, off one's guard.

inquam, inquit, say.

insequor, -secutus (3), follow.

insidiae, -arum, *f. pl.*, ambush; treachery.

insidiator, -oris, *m.*, brigand, waylayer.

insidior (1), lie in ambush.

insigne, -is, *n.*, *in pl.*, regalia.

insignis, -e, distinguished, prominent.

insolens, -ntis, unaccustomed (to).

instituo, -ui, -utum (3), begin.

insto, -stiti, -statum (1), press on, press forward, threaten.

instruo, -uxi, -uctum (3), supply; draw up, marshal (*troops*).

insula, -ae, *f.*, island.

intactus, -a, -um, untouched, intact, uninjured.

integer, -gra, -grum, fresh, unwounded (*Caesar*); untouched, whole (*Cicero*).

intellego, -lexi, -lectum (3), understand, perceive, realise.

intendo, -di, -tum (3), aim; *with infin.*, intend.

inter, *prep. with acc.*, among, between.

intercedo, -cessi, -cessum (3), come between; (*of time*) intervene.

interdum, *adv.*, sometimes.

intereo, -ire, -ivi *or* -ii, -itum, am lost, am killed.

interest, -esse, -fuit, it is of importance, it concerns.

interficio, -ere, -feci, -fectum, kill, put to death.

interim, *adv.*, meanwhile.

internuntius, -i, *m.*, mediator, go between.

interpono, -posui, -positum (3), introduce ; se interponere, act as an agent.

interpres, -pretis, *m.*, interpreter.

interrumpo, -rupi, -ruptum (3), break down.

intersero (3), allege (*a pretext or reason*).

intersum, -esse, -fui, +*dat.*, take part in.

intervallum, -i, *n.*, interval, distance.

intervenio, -veni, -ventum (4), stand in the way ; oppose.

intra, *prep. with acc.*, within, inside.

intro (1), enter.

intueor (2), gaze at.

inultus, -a, -um, unavenged.

invado, -si, -sum (3), seize, lay hold of ; attack.

invenio, -veni, -ventum (4), (come upon), find.

inviolatus, -a, -um, unhurt.

invitus, -a, -um, unwilling, against one's will.

Iones, -um, *m. pl.*, Ionians (*Greek inhabitants of Ionia*).

Ionia, -ae, *f.*, Ionia (*part of Asia Minor bordering on Aegean Sea*).

Iovem, *acc.*, of Iupiter.

ipse, -a, -um, -self, he himself ; herself ; itself, etc.

ira, -ae, *f.*, anger.

is, ea, id, that ; he, she, it, etc. ; such.

iste, -a, -ud, that (*of yours*).

ita, *adv.*, so, thus, in such a way ; thereon.

itaque, *adv.*, and so, therefore, accordingly.

iter, itineris, *n.*, way, passage ; route, march, journey, road.

iterum, *adv.*, a second time.

Iuba, -ae, *m.*, Juba, king of Numidia (*North Africa*).

iubeo, iussi, iussum (2), order, bid, command.

iudex, -icis, *m.*, (judge), juryman.

iudico (1), judge, decide.

Iugurtha, -ae, *m.*, Jugurtha (*prince of the royal house of Numidia*).

iure, *adv.*, rightfully, with justice.

Iupiter, Iovem, Iovis, etc., *m.*, Jupiter, chief of the gods.

ius, iuris, *n.*, right, law.

(iussus), *abl.*, iussu (4), command, order.

iustitia, -ae, *f.*, justice.

iustus, -a, -um, proper.

iuvenis, -is, *m.*, a youth, a young man.

iuventa, -ae, *f.*, youth.

iuventus, -utis, *f.*, youth, young men.

iuvo, iuvi, iutum (1), help, aid, support ; *impersonally*, it delights, pleases (*Livy, Scaevola*).

K

Kalendae, -arum, *f. pl.*, Kalends (*first day of the month*).

L

labor, -oris, *m.*, work ; effort, exertion.

Lacedaemon, -onis, *f.*, Lacedaemon, Sparta.

Lacedaemonius, -i, *m.*, a Lacedaemonian, Spartan ; *also as adj.*, Spartan.

lacrimo (1), weep.

laedo, -si, -sum (3), hurt, sully.

laetor (1), rejoice at, be pleased.

laetus, -a, -um, glad, joyful.

lamenta, -orum, *n. pl.*, wailing, weeping, lament.

Lanuvinus, -i, *m.*, native of Lanuvium.

Lanuvium, -i, *n.*, Lanuvium, town in Latium.

Larcius (Spurius), *m.*, Spurius Larcius.

largitio, -ionis, *f.*, generous award, granting.

lassitudo, -inis, *f.*, weariness.

Latini, -orum, *m. pl.*, Latins (natives of Latium).

latro, -onis, *m.*, brigand.

laudo (1), praise.

laus, laudis, *f.*, praise (*Caesar*) ; fame, renown (*Nepos*).

legatus, -i, *m.*, envoy, representative.

legio, -ionis, *f.*, legion.

legitimus, -a, -um, lawful, usual.

lego, legi, lectum (3), pick up, collect (*Livy*) ; read (*Cicero*).

lenio (4), soothe, appease ; *in pass.*, give way.

lente, *adv.*, slowly.

lenunculus, -i, *m.*, skiff.

libenter, *adv.*, gladly.

liber, -era, -erum, free.

liberalitas, -tatis, *f.*, generosity.

libere, *adv.*, freely, unrestrictedly.

liberi, -orum, *m. pl.*, children.

libero (1), free, liberate.

libertas, -tatis, *f.*, freedom, liberty.

libet (2), *impersonal*, it pleases, it is agreeable.

libido, -inis, *f.*, (personal) inclination.

licenter, *adv.* (*comp.*, licentius), freely, without restraint.

licet (2), it is allowed, one may.

lingua, -ae, *f.*, tongue, language.

lis, litis, *f.*, damages.

litterae, -arum, *f. pl.*, letter, despatch.

loco (1), play, put, pitch.

litus, -oris, *n.*, shore, beach.

locus, -i, *m.*, *sometimes n. in pl.*, place, spot, ground, district, region ; position, rank (*Cicero*).

longe, *adv.*, afar, far off; away; *comp.*,l ongius.

longus, -a, -um, long.

loquor, locutus (3), say, speak.

luctus, -us(4), grief, sorrow.

lucus, -i (2 , grove, wood.

lux, lucis, *f.*, light ; dawn, day

M

maeror, -oris, *m.*, grief, sadness.

magis, *adv.*, more, rather.

magister, -tri, *m.*, master, captain.

magistratus, -us, *m.*, magistracy.

magnitudo, -inis, *f.*, greatness, magnitude.

magnopere, *adv.*, greatly.

magnus, -a, -um, great ; *comp.*, maior, *superl.*, maximus.

maiestas, -tatis, *f.*, dignity.

male, *adv.*, badly ; unsuccessfully.

malo, malle, malui, prefer, choose.

malum, -i, *n.*, evil, calamity, misfortune.

mancus, -a, -um, crippled, ineffective.

maneo, mansi, mansum (2), stay, remain.

manus, -us, *f.*, hand ; band, force ; manu, by force (*Sallust*).

Marathon, -onis, *f.*, Marathon (*a town near the eastern coast of Attica*).

Marathonius, -a, -um, of Marathon.

Marcius, -i, *m.*, Marcius.

mare, -is, *n.*, sea.

Marius, -i, *m.*, Marius (*commander-in-chief of the Roman troops operating against Jugurtha*).

Massugrada, -ae, *m.*, Massugrada (*a Numidian of the royal family*).

mater, matris, *f.*, mother.

materia, -ae, *f.*, timber.

Maurus, -i, *m.*, the Moor = *either* Volux *or* Bocchus ; *as adj.*, Moorish.

maxime, *superl. adv.*, most, especially.

maximus, -a, -um, *see* magnus.

medicina, -ae, *f.*, remedy, relief.

mediocris, -e, mean, ordinary ; small (*Caesar*).

medius, -a, -um, mid, middle ; *as noun in n. sg.*, medium, -i, middle.

me hercule, by Hercules, assuredly.

memini, -isse, remember.

mensis, -is, *m.*, month.

mentior (4), lie, assert falsely.

meritum, -i, *n.*, service.

metor (1), lay out, pitch (*a camp*).

metuo, -ui (3), fear.

metus, -us (4), fear.

meus, -a, -um, my.

miles, -itis, *m.*, soldier.

Milesius, -a, -um, of Miletus (*town in Asia Minor*).

milia, -ium, *plural of* mille ; milia passuum, miles.

militaris, -e, military, fit for service ; res militaris, the art of war, warfare.

mille, a thousand.

Milo, -onis, *m.*, Milo (*bitter rival of Clodius*).

Miltiades, -is, *m.*, Miltiades (*Athenian general*)

mina, -ae, *f.*, threat.

minaciter, *adv.*, threateningly, menacingly.

minime, *superl. adv.*, by no means, not at all.

minitabundus, -a, -um, threatening.

minuo, -ui, -utum (3), lesson, diminish.

minus, *adv.*, less, the less.

mirabilis, -e, wonderful.

miraculum, -i, *n.*, miracle.

mirus, -a, -um, wonderful.

misceo, -cui, -xtum (2), mix, mingle.

miser, -era, -erum, helpless.

miserabilis, -e, piteous.

misericordia, -ae, *f.*, pity, compassion.

miseror (1), deplore.

mitto, misi, missum (3), send.

modice, *adv.*, modestly.

modicus, -a, -um, moderate, ordinary, small.

modo, *adv.*, only ; modo . . . modo, now . . . now.

moenia, -ium, *n. pl.*, (city) walls.

moneo (2), warn, advise.

mons, montis, *m.*, hill, mountain.

morior, -i, mortuus, die.

moror (1), delay.

mors, mortis, *f.*, death.

mortalis, -e, mortal ; *as noun*, a mortal.

mortuus, -a, -um, dead.

mos, moris, *m.*, manner, custom ; *in pl.*, character.

moveo, movi, motum (2), move ; arouse (*anger*) ; affect, stir.

mox, *adv.*, soon, presently.

Mucius, -i, *m.*, Gaius Mucius (*Scaevola*).

mucro, -onis, *m.*, (sword's point), sword.

muliebris, -e, of women.

multitudo, -inis, *f.*, crowd, large numbers, host ; people, populace ; superior numbers.

multo, *adv.*, by far, much.

multo (1), punish.

multum, *adv.*, much ; frequently (*Sallust*).

multus, -a, -um, much ; *in pl.*, many.

Muluccha, -ae, *m.*, river in Numidia, N. Africa.

munimentum, -i, *n.*, protection.

munio (4), fortify, guard, secure,

munitio, -ionis, *f.*, fortification. entrenchment.

murus, -i, *m.*, wall.

muto (1), change.

N

nam, *conj.*, for.

namque, *conj.*, for.

nanciscor, nactus (3), get, obtain.

nascor, natus (3), be born.

natura, -ae, *f.*, nature.

natus, -i, *m.*, son.

navis, -is, *f.*, ship, boat.

ne, lest, (in order) that . . . not ; ne . . . quidem, not even.

nec, *see* neque ; nec . . . nec, neither . . . nor.

necessarius, -a, -um, necessary.

necessarius, -i, *m.*, friend.

necesse, *neut. only*, necessary.

necessitas, -tatis, *f.*, necessity.

negito (1), keep on saying 'no '.

nego (1), deny, say that . . . not.

negotium, -i, *n.*, business, matter ; trouble.

nemo, *acc.*, neminem, *gen.*, nullius, *dat.*, nemini, *abl.*, nullo, no-one, nobody.

nequaquam, *adv.*, in no wise, not at all.

neque, and not, but not, nor ; neque . . . neque, neither . . . nor.

nequeo, -ire, be unable, cannot.

nequiquam, *adv.*, in vain, to no purpose.

nescio (4), know not.

neu *or* neve, nor, and not.

ni = nisi, unless.

nihil, *n.*, *indecl.*, nothing.

nihilum, -i, *n.*, nothing.

nisi, if not, unless ; except.

nitor, nisus *or* nixus (3), strive,

struggle; *with abl.*, rely or rest on.

nobilis, -e, high-born, distinguished.

noctu, by night.

nocturnus, -a, -um, in the night, by night.

nomen, -inis, *n.*, name.

non, not.

non nullus, -a, -um, some.

noster, -tra, -trum, our; *m. pl.*, nostri, -orum, our men.

notus, -a, -um, known.

novi (*perf. of* nosco), I know.

novus, -a, -um, new; novissimum agmen, the rear.

nox, noctis, *f.*, night.

nullus, -a, -um, no, not any.

numerus, -i, *m.*, number; *abl.*, numero, =as.

Numida, -ae, *m.*, a Numidian; *in Sallust often* =Jugurtha.

Numidia, -ae, *f.*, Numidia.

numquam, *adv.*, never.

nunc, *adv.*, now; nunc ... nunc, now ... now.

nuntio (1), announce, report.

nuntius, -i, *m.*, messenger; message, report.

nusquam, *adv.*, nowhere.

O

ob, *prep. with acc.*, on account of.

obeo, -ire, -ii, -itum, meet (*Cicero*); die.

obicio, -ere, -ieci, -iectum, throw in the way of; hold in front (*of shields*).

obscurus, -a, -um, obscure, unintelligible.

obsecro (1), pray.

obsideo, -sedi, -sessum (2), besiege, beset, blockade.

obsidio, -onis, *f.*, siege, blockade.

obsisto, -stiti, -stitum (3), oppose, resist.

obsoletus, a, -um, common.

obstinatus, -a, -um, obstinate, firm.

obsto, -stiti, (1), hinder, oppose.

obstupefacio, -ere, -feci, -factum, amaze.

obstupefactus, -a, -um, thunderstruck, amazed.

obtesto (1), call as a witness (*Sallust*); entreat, beseech (*Livy*).

obtineo, -tinui, -tentum (2), hold, occupy.

obtrunco (1), cut down, kill, slaughter.

obverto, -ti, -sum (3), turn towards, direct against.

obviam, *adv.*, to meet; obviam fio, *with dat.*, meet.

obvius, -a, -um, meeting, to meet.

occasio, -ionis, *f.*, opportunity, chance.

occasus, -us, *m.*, setting (*of the sun*); solis occasus, sun-set.

occido, -cidi, -cisum (3), kill, slay.

occulte, *adv.*, secretly.

occupatio, -ionis, *f.*, business.

occurro, -curri, -cursum (3), appear, occur.

occursus, -us (4), a meeting, a falling in with.

octavus, -a, -um, eighth.

oculus, -i, *m.*, eye; *in pl.*, gaze, looks.

offensio, -ionis, f., disgust.

officium, -i, n., duty (Caesar); allegiance (Nepos).

olim, adv., once, formerly.

omitto, -misi, -missum (3), give up.

omnino, adv., at all.

omnis, -e, every, all.

onerarius, -a, -um, of burden; navis oneraria, merchant ship.

onero (1), burden.

onus, -eris, n., load, weight.

opera, -ae, f., labour, work (Cicero); assistance (Sallust); operam do, take pains, give attention to.

(ops), f., acc., opem, gen., opis, help, aid; in pl., resources, power.

opinio, -ionis, f., expectation (Caesar); belief (Nepos).

oppidanus, -i, m., townsman.

oppidum, -i, n., town.

opportunus, -a, -um, convenient, suitable.

opprimo, -pressi, -pressum (3), crush, overwhelm.

oppugnator, -oris, m., besieger.

oppugno (1), attack.

optimus, -a, -um, superl. of bonus, best, very good.

opto (1), wish, long for.

opus, -eris, n., work, task; work (of siege or defence); opus est, there is need.

oratio, -ionis, f., speech, discourse; report.

orator, -toris, m., legate, negotiator.

orbo (1), with abl., deprive or bereave of.

ordo, -inis, m., order, discipline

(Caesar); rank, line (Caesar, Livy).

orior, ortus (4), rise.

ornatus, -us (4), dress, apparel, garb.

oro (1), beg, pray.

ortus, -us, m., rising.

ostendo, -di, -sum or -tum (3), show; se ostendere, appear.

ostento (1), show off, boast, vaunt.

otium, -i, n., peace.

P

Paelignus, -a, -um, Pelignian (tribe in Central Italy).

paene, adv., almost, nearly.

paenitet (2), imperson., repent.

paenula, -ae, f., travelling cloak.

paenulatus, -a, -um, in travelling dress.

palam, adv., openly, publicly.

Palatium, -i, n., the Palatine Hill.

Papirius, -i, m., Papirius.

par, paris, equal.

paratus, -a, -um, ready, prepared, determined.

parco, peperci, parsum (3), with dat., spare.

parens, -ntis, c., parent, father.

pariter, adv., alike, equally; at the same time.

Parius, -a, -um, Parian, of Paros; as noun, native of Paros.

paro (1), prepare, get ready.

pars, partis, f., part; party (political) (Cicero); pars ... pars, some ... others.

partim, *adv.*, partly ; **partim** . . . **partim,** partly . . . partly.

parum, *adv.*, too little, insufficiently, not enough.

parumper, *adv.*, a little, for a little while.

parvus, minor, minimus, small.

passim, *adv.*, indiscriminately.

passus, -us, *m.*, pace ; mille **passus,** a mile.

patefacio, -facere, -feci, -factum, disclose.

patens, -ntis, open.

pateo, (2), be open ; available (*Nepos*).

pater, -tris, *m.*, father ; *in pl.*, the fathers, the senate ; pater **familiae,** a civilian.

patior, -i, passus, suffer.

pauci, -ae, -a, few.

paulatim, *adv.*, gradually.

paulisper, *adv.*, a little while.

paveo, pavi (2), be frightened, terrified, alarmed.

pavide, *adv.*, fearfully, with fear.

pavor, -oris, *m.*, fear.

pecunia, -ae, *f.*, money.

pedes, -itis, *m.*, footsoldier ; *in pl.*, infantry.

peditatus, -us, *m.*, infantry.

pendeo, pependi (2), (hang), be dependent.

penetro (1), enter, penetrate.

per, *prep. with acc.*, through, along, over ; by means of ; **per se,** of themselves.

percutio, -ere, -cussi, -cussum, strike.

perditus, -a, -um, lost, hopeless, desperate ; abandoned, wicked (*Cicero*).

perdo, -didi, -ditum (3), destroy, lose.

pereo, -ire, -ii, -itum, be lost, perish.

perfero, -ferre, -tuli, -latum, convey.

perficio, -ere, -feci, -fectum, complete, finish, accomplish.

perfidia, -ae, *f.*, treachery.

perfuga, -ae, *m.*, deserter, refugee.

periculum, -i, *n.*, danger, risk, peril.

permagnus, -a, -um, very great.

permoveo, -movi, -motum (2), alarm, agitate.

permulceo, -lsi, -lsum (2), stroke.

perpauci, -ae, -a, very few.

perpetuus, -a, -um, unbroken, constant.

Persa, -ae, *m.*, a Persian.

persequor, -secutus (3), follow, attend ; bello persequi, hunt down (*Nepos*).

perterreo (2), alarm, terrify, strike with panic.

pertimesco, -mui (3), fear.

pertinacia, -ae, *f.*, obstinacy.

perturbo (1), wreck.

pervenio, -veni, -ventum (4), reach, arrive.

pes, pedis, *m.*, foot; **pedem referre,** give ground, retreat.

petitio, -ionis, *f.*, canvassing, candidature.

peto, -ivi, -itum (3), seek ; aim at, make for ; demand, entreat (*Sallust*).

Philippides, *m.*, Philippides (*long distance runner*).

pietas, -tatis, *f.*, filial affection.

Pisistratus, -i, *m.*, Pisistratus (*tyrant of Athens*).

placeo (2), please ; *impersonally*, it pleases, =decide.

Plataeenses, -ium, *m. pl.*, Plataeans (*natives of Plataea*).

plebs, plebis, *f.*, the people, plebs.

plecto (3), *only in passive*, be punished.

plenus, -a, -um, full (*with gen. or abl.*, *in Caesar*).

plerique, -aeque, -aque, very many, the majority, most.

plerumque, *n.*, most (*followed by partitive gen.*).

plurimum, *adv.*, *superl. of* multum, very much, most.

plurimus, -a, -um, *superl. of* multus, very many.

plus, pluris, *n.*, *only in sg.*, more ; **plures, -a,** more.

Poecile, -es, *f.*, picture gallery (*in Athens*).

poena, -ae, *f.*, retribution, satisfaction.

polliceor (2), promise.

pono, posui, positum (3), put, place, station.

pons, pontis, *m.*, bridge ; **pons sublicius,** bridge of piles.

populatio, -ionis, *f.*, plundering, ravaging.

populus, -i, *m.*, people, populace ; nation.

porta, -ae, *f.*, gate, door.

porticus, -us, *m.*, porch.

porro, *adv.*, furthermore.

Porsinna, -ae, *m.*, Porsinna.

possum, posse, potui, am able, can.

post, *prep. with acc.*, after, behind ; *as adverb*, afterwards, later ; behind.

postea, *adv.*, afterwards.

posteaquam, *conj.*, after.

posterus, -a, -um, following, next ; **posteri, -orum,** *m. pl.*, posterity.

postquam, *conj.*, after, when.

postremo, *adv.*, finally.

postulo (1), ask, demand.

potentia, -ae, *f.*, power.

potestas, -tatis, *f.*, power, control.

potior (4), *with abl.*, gain possession of.

potius, rather.

prae, *prep. with abl.*, before ; **prae se ferre,** to display, parade.

praecipio, -ere, -cepi, -ceptum, instruct.

praeclare, *adv.*, splendidly, wonderfully.

praeda, -ae, *f.*, booty, plunder, prize.

praedico (1), declare, speak, talk, assert.

praedico, -dixi, -dictum (3), warn, command.

praedo, -onis, *m.*, robber, brigand.

praefectus, -i, *m.*, commander.

praefero, -ferre, -tuli, -latum, display.

praeficio, -ere, -feci, -fectum, put in command.

praegredior, -i, -gressus, go on, advance.

praemitto, -misi, -missum (3), send on, send ahead.

praemium, -i, *n.,* reward, recompense.

praeoccupo (1), seize first.

praescribo, -psi, -ptum (3), teach, ordain.

praesens, -ntis, present ; *with* **animus,** resolute.

praesentia, -ae, *f.,* presence ; **in praesentia,** at the time.

praesertim, *adv.,* especially.

praesidium, -i, *n.,* protection ; garrison, detachment, post.

praesum, -esse, -fui, *with dat.,* be in command of.

praeter, *prep. with acc.,* besides, in addition to ; except.

praeterea, *adv.,* besides, in addition.

praetermitto, -misi, -missum, omit.

praetor, -oris, *m.,* general.

praetura, -ae, *f.,* office of praetor, praetorship.

precem, -is (*no nom.*), *f.,* entreaty.

precor (1), entreat, beg, pray.

premo, pressi, pressum (3), press hard, harass.

pretium, -i, *n.,* price.

pridie, *adv.,* on the day before ; on the previous day.

primo, *adv.,* at first, firstly.

primum, *adv.,* first, at first.

primus, -a, -um, first.

princeps, -ipis, *m.,* chief, leading man.

prior, -ius, earlier, previous, former.

pristinus, -a, -um, former.

priusquam, *conj.,* before.

privatus, -a, -um, private ; *as noun,* a private citizen.

privo (1), deprive (of).

pro, *prep. with abl.,* before, in front of ; in place of, instead of ; on behalf of (*Sallust and Livy*) ; in return for (*Caesar, Chap.* 36).

probo (1), approve.

procedo, -cessi, -cessum (3), go forward, advance.

procella, -ae, *f.,* storm.

procer, -eris, *m., usually in pl.,* leading men, chiefs, nobles.

procul, *adv.,* afar, far off ; in the distance (*Caesar*).

procumbo, -cubui, cubitum (3), sink down.

procurro, -cucurri *and* **-curri, -cursum** (3), run forward.

proditio, -ionis, *f.,* treachery.

prodo, -didi, -ditum (3), betray ; nominate (*Cicero*).

produco, -xi, -ctum (3), bring out (*Caesar*) ; lead forth.

proelior (1), fight.

proelium, -i, *n.,* battle, fight.

profecto, *adv.,* assuredly.

proficiscor, -fectus (3), set out, start.

profligo (1), crush, shatter, defeat.

profugio, -ere, -fugi, -fugitum, flee, take to flight.

progredior, -i, -gressus, advance.

prohibeo (2), prevent, hinder, stop ; defend, protect (*Sallust*).

proinde, *adv.,* therefore.

promitto, -misi, -missum (3), promise.

promptus (4), *only in abl.,* **in promptu esse,** to be easy.

prope, *prep. with acc.*, near ; *as adv.*, near ; nearly, almost ; *comp.*, propius ; *superl.*, proxime.

propere, *adv.*, quickly, speedily.

propero (1), hasten (*intrans.*) ; quicken, accelerate (*transitive, Sallust*).

propinquitas, -tatis, *f.*, nearness, proximity.

propinquus, -a, -um, neighbouring, near.

propitius, -a, -um, favourable, propitious.

propius, *see* prope *as adv.*

propulso (1), ward off, repel.

prosequor, -secutus (3), follow, attend ; pursue (*Caesar*).

prosilio, -ui (4), leap from *or* forward.

prosterno, -stravi, -stratum (3), overthrow, destroy.

prosum, -desse, -fui, *with dat.*, be advantageous to.

protero, —, -tritum, (3), trample down.

proventus, -us (4), success.

provoco (1), challenge.

proximus, -a, -um, next, following ; nearest.

prudentia, -ae, *f.*, discretion, wisdom.

publicus, -a, -um, public.

pudor, -oris, *m.*, shame.

puer, -eri, *m.*, boy ; page (*Cicero, Pro Milone*).

pugna, -ae, *f.*, fight, combat.

pugno (1), fight.

pulvis, -eris, *m.*, dust.

Punicus, -a, -um, Punic, Carthaginian.

puto (1), think.

Q

qua, *rel. adv.*, where ; whereby.

quadriduum, -i, *n.*, (a period of) four days.

quaero, -sivi, -situm (3), seek, search for, ask.

quaestor, -oris, *m.*, quaestor.

qualis, -e, *interrog.*, what sort of?

quam, *adv. and conj.*, how ; than (*after comparat.*) ; *with superl. adj. or adv.*, as . . . as possible.

quam ob rem, wherefore.

quamquam, *conj.*, although.

quamvis, *conj.*, although.

quando, *conj.*, since.

quantus, -a, -um, how much? how big? ; *correl.*, as much as.

qua re, *adv.*, wherefore.

quartus, -a, -um, fourth.

quasi, *adv.*, as if.

-que, *enclitic conj.*, and.

queror, questus (3), complain.

qui, quae, quod, *rel. pron.*, who which, what, that which.

quia, *conj.*, because.

qui-, quae-, quodcumque, whoever, whichever, whatever.

quid (*neut. of* quis), *adv.*, why? how?

quidam, quaedam, quoddam, a, a certain ; a kind of.

quidem, *adv.*, indeed ; ne . . . quidem, not even.

quietus, -a, -um, calm, peaceful.

quin, *conj.*, but that, that not, without ; *as adv.*, nay more, furthermore.

quingenti, -ae, -a, five hundred.

quinquaginta, fifty.

quintus, -a, -um, fifth.

quippe, *conj.*, for, since.

quis, quid, *interrog. pron.,* who? which? what?

quis, qua, quid, *indefinite pron.,* anyone, anything ; ne quis, that no-one.

quisnam, quaenam, quidnam, *interrog. pron.,* who then? who pray?

quisquam, quidquam, *or* **quicquam,** any, anyone, anything.

quisque, quaeque, quidque, each, every. a man.

quisquis, quidquid (quicquid), whoever, whatever.

quo, *interrog. and relative adv.,* whither, to which, where.

quo, *conj. used with comparatives,* in order that.

quoad, *conj.,* until, as long as.

quod, *conj.,* because.

quondam *adv.,* formerly, once.

quoniam, *conj.,* since, as.

quoque, *adv.,* also, too.

R

radix, -icis, *f.,* root, foot.

raeda, -ae, *f.,* carriage.

raedarius, -i, *m.,* driver.

rarus, -a, -um, at wide intervals, infrequent.

ratio, -ionis, *f.,* plan, reason.

ratus, -a, -um, established, settled.

recipio, -ere, -cepi, -ceptum, take in, take on board (*Caesar*) ; se recipere, retreat, retire.

reconcilio (1), recover.

recreo (1), refresh, revive.

recte, *adv.,* rightly.

recurro, -curri, -cursum (3), run *or* hasten.

reddo, -didi, -ditum (3), repay.

redeo, -ire, -ii, -itum, return.

redigo, -egi, -actum (3), reduce.

reduco, -duxi, -ductum (3), lead back, withdraw (*Caesar*) ; escort (*Cicero*).

refero, -ferre, rettuli, relatum, bring back ; report ; pedem referre, give ground, retreat ; gratiam referre, return thanks, show gratitude.

refert, retulit, *impersonal,* it concerns, it is of importance.

refertus, -a, -um, crammed, filled, crowded.

reficio, -ere, -feci, -fectum, refresh, rest.

refugio, -ere, -fugi, -fugitum, flee back.

regia, -ae, *f.,* palace.

regio, -ionis, *f.,* ground.

regius, -a, -um, royal.

regnum, -i, *n.,* kingdom, rule, sovereignty.

regredior, -i, -gressus, go back, return.

reiectus, -a, -um, thrown over (*of a cloak*).

religio, -ionis, *f.,* religious scruple.

relinquo, -liqui, -lictum (3), leave, leave behind, abandon.

reliquus, -a, -um, remaining ; *in pl.,* the rest, the other.

reor, ratus (2), think.

remitto, -misi, -missum (3), send back.

removeo, -movi, -motum (2), send away.

remuneror (1), repay.

repello, reppuli, repulsum (3), drive back, reject, repulse.

repente, *adv.,* suddenly.

repentinus, -a, -um, sudden.

reperio, repperi, repertum (4), learn, discover.

repono, -posui, -positum (3), place.

reporto (1), carry back.

reprehenso (1), keep holding back.

res, rei, *f.*, matter, business, affair, deed ; res publica, state, commonwealth.

rescindo, -scidi, -scissum (3), cut *or* break down.

resisto, -stiti, -stitum (3), halt, stay behind ; resist (*with dat.*).

respicio, -ere, -spexi, -spectum, look back (at) (*Caesar*) ; regard, be mindful (of) (*Nepos*).

respondeo, -di, -sum (2), answer, reply.

restituo, -ui, -utum (3), restore, re-establish.

retineo, -tinui, -tentum (2), detain, keep.

retraho, -traxi, -tractum (3), drag back.

revertor, *perf.*, reverti, turn back, return.

revoco (1), recall.

rex, regis, *m.*, king, prince.

robur, -oris, *n.*, flower, pick.

rogito (1), ask repeatedly, keep asking.

rogo (1), ask.

Roma, -ae, *f.*, Rome.

Romanus, -a, -um, Roman ; *as noun*, a Roman.

Rufus, -i, *m.*, Rufus.

ruina, -ae, *f.*, downfall, destruction.

rumpo, rupi, ruptum (3), break.

ruo, rui, rutum (3), rush.

rursus, *adv.*, again.

S

Saburra, -ae, *m.*, Saburra.

sacerdos, -otis, *m. or f.*, priest *or* priestess.

sacra, -orum, *n. pl.*, sacred vessels.

sacrificium, -i, *n.*, sacrifice.

saepe, *adv.*, often.

saepio, -psi, -ptum (4), surround, enclose ; fortify.

sagittarius, -i, *m.*, archer.

sal, salis, *m.*, salt.

salinum, -i, *n.*, salt-pan.

salus, -utis, *f.*, safety, deliverance, life.

Sampsiceramus, -i, *m.*, the Nabob (*a playful name for Pompey*).

sancte, *adv.*, reverently, solemnly.

sanctus, -a, -um, upright.

sane, *adv.*, indeed, doubtless.

sapiens, -ntis, *m.*, a philosopher.

Sardes, -ium, *f. pl.*, Sardis (*important town in Asia Minor*).

satelles, -itis, *m.*, attendant.

satis, *adv.*, enough, sufficiently.

scapha, -ae, *f.*, boat.

scelus, -eris, *n.*, crime.

scio (4), know.

scipio, -ionis, *m.*, staff.

Scipio, -ionis, *m.*, Scipio (the Younger).

sciscitor (1), ask, enquire.

scriba, -ae, *m.*, clerk.

scribo, scripsi, scriptum (3), write.

scutum, -i, *n.*, shield.

Scythia, -ae, *f.*, Scythia.

se *or* sese, himself, themselves.

secundus, -a, -um, successful.

secus, *adv.*, otherwise.

sed, but.

sedeo, sedi, sessum (2), sit ; remain encamped.

sedes, -is, *f.*, seat.

sella, -ae, *f.*, seat, chair.

semet, *pronoun, stronger form of* se.

senator, -oris, *m.*, senator.

senatus, -us, *m.*, senate.

senectus, -utis, *f.*, old age.

senex, senis, *m.*, old man.

senior, -ioris, *m.*, old *or* older man.

sensus, -us, *m.*, sensation ; pain (*Cicero, De Amicitia*).

sententia, -ae, *f.*, proposal (*Nepos*) ; opinion (*Sallust*) ; vote (*Cicero*).

sentio, sensi, sensum (4), perceive, realise.

septuaginta (*indecl.*), seventy.

sequor, secutus (3), follow.

sermo, -onis, *m.*, talk, conversation.

sero, *adv.*, too late.

servitium, -i, *n.*, tool, chattel.

servo (1), save.

servus, -i, *m.*, slave.

sese = se.

sexaginta, *indecl.*, sixty.

si, if.

sic, *adv.*, so, thus, in this manner

Sicilia, -ae, *f.*, Sicily.

sicuti, just as.

significo (1), signify, declare, indicate.

signum, -i, *n.*, sign, signal ; (military) standard (*Caesar*).

silentium, -i, *n.*, silence.

silva, -ae, *f.*, wood, forest.

similis, -e, like.

simul, *adv.*, at the same time.

simulacrum, -i, *n.*, statue.

simulatio, -ionis, *f.*, pretence.

simulo (1), pretend, simulate.

sin, but if.

sine, *prep. with abl.*, without.

singularis, -e, outstanding, remarkable.

singuli, -ae, -a, one each, single, individual.

sino, sivi, situm (3), allow.

situs, -us, *m.*, site, position.

socius, -i, *m.*, friend, supporter.

sol, solis, *m.*, sun.

solacium, -i, *n.*, consolation.

soleo, solitus sum (2), am accustomed.

solitudo, -inis, *f.*, solitude ; desert, wilderness.

sollemnis, -e, yearly.

solum, *adv.*, only.

solus, -a, -um, alone, only.

solvo, -vi, solutum (3), pay.

somnus, -i, *m.*, sleep.

soror, -oris, *f.*, sister.

sors, sortis, *f.*, lot.

species, -ei, *f.*, appearance, sight, show.

specto (1), look at *or* to.

speculator, -oris, *m.*, scout ; *in pl.*, patrol.

speculor (1), observe, watch.

spes, -ei, *f.*, hope, expectation.

spolium, -i, *n.*, *usually in pl.*, spoils, trophies.

sponte, *abl., sing. fem., no nom.*, sponte sua, of one's own accord, voluntarily.

statim, *adv.*, at once.

statio, -ionis, *f.*, guard, picket, outpost.

statua, -ae, *f.*, statue.

statuo, -ui, -utum (3), determine ; erect (*Nepos*).

status, -us, *m.*, rank, position.

Stesagoras, -ae, *m.*, Stesagoras (*brother of Miltiades*).

stipendium, -i, *n.*, pay.

sto, steti, statum (1), stand.

strenuus, -a, -um, active, vigorous.

studium, -i, *n.*, enthusiasm.

stupefacio, -ere, -feci, -factum, stun, stupefy.

suadeo, -si, -sum (2), advise, urge.

sub, *prep. with acc.*, (*of time*) towards, about ; *prep. with abl.*, under, below, close to.

subdole, *adv.*, craftily.

subeo, -ire, -ii, -itum, go under ; *with* casum, take a chance.

subito, *adv.*, suddenly.

subitus, -a, -um, sudden.

sublicius, -a, -um, of piles ; pons sublicius, the pile-bridge (*across the Tiber*).

subsequor, -secutus (3), follow closely, keep up.

subsidium, -i, *n.*, help, support, relief.

subsisto, -stiti, -stitum (3), stay behind, halt, stop.

succurro, -curri, -cursum (3), *with dat.*, help, assist.

suffragium, -i, *n.*, vote.

Sulla, -ae, *m.*, Sulla (*quaestor of Marius*).

sum, esse, fui, am.

summa, -ae, *f.*, chief part.

summitto, -misi, -missum (3), send up, send in support of ; send to the relief of.

summum, *adv.*, at the most (*Cicero*).

summus, -a, -um, highest, greatest, very great.

sumo, -mpsi, -mptum, (3), take.

sumptus, -us (4), expense.

superbus, -a, -um, proud.

superincido (3), fall from above.

superior, -ioris, higher, former, previous.

supero (1), overcome, defeat, surpass.

supersum, -esse, -fui, be left ; survive.

superus, -a, -um, above.

supremus, -a, -um, last.

suspensus, -a, -um, in suspense.

suspicor (1), suspect ; anticipate (*Caesar*).

sustineo, -tinui, -tentum (2), stop, check ; withstand, resist (*Livy*) ; uphold (*Cicero*).

suus, -a, -um, his (own), their (own).

T

talentum, -i, *n.*, a talent (about £233).

talis, -e, such, of such a kind.

tam, so.

tamen, *adv.*, but, yet, nevertheless.

tandem, *adv.*, at last.

tanto, (by) so much.

tantum modo, *adv.*, only.

tantus, -a, -um, so much, so great.

tardo (1) delay ; *in pass.*, be slow.

tardus, -a, -um, slow.

tectum, -i, n., house, dwelling.

tego, texi, tectum (3), cover, protect.

telum, -i, n., missile, weapon, spear, javelin.

temere, adv., rashly, by chance; recklessly (Sallust).

tempestas, -tatis, f., time.

templum, -i, n., temple.

tempto (1), try.

tempus, -oris, n., time; chance, opportunity; hour, moment (Caesar).

tendo, tetendi, tensum (2), lay, contrive (an ambush).

teneo, -nui, -ntum (2), hold; detain (Livy, Hannibal); check (Livy, Gauls); keep.

tensa, -ae, f., car, chariot (of the gods).

tenuis, -e, rare.

tergum, -i, n., back; a tergo, in the rear.

terra, -ae, f., land, country.

terror, -oris, m., terror, panic.

testis, -is, m., witness.

testor (1), invoke, appeal to.

testudo, -inis, f., pent house.

Tiberinus, -a, -um, of the Tiber.

Tiberis, -is, m., the river Tiber.

timeo (2), am afraid, fear.

timor, -oris, m., fear, dread.

tollo, sustuli, sublatum (3), raise; in pass., be elated (Caesar).

torreo, torrui, tostum (2), scorch, burn.

totidem, just as many.

totiens, adv., so often, so many times.

totus, -a, -um, the whole, entire.

tractus, -us (4), hauling, dragging.

trado, -didi, -ditum (3), hand over, betray.

traduco, -duxi, -ductum (3), take across.

traho, traxi, tractum (3), draw (Nepos); drag, lead (Livy); delay (Cicero).

traicio, -ere, -ieci, -iectum, take across.

trano (1), swim across.

transeo, -ire, -ii, -itum, cross.

transfero, -ferre, -tuli, -latum, transfer.

transfuga, -ae, m., deserter.

transporto (1), carry across.

trecenti, -ae, -a, three hundred.

trepidus, -a, -um, fearful, in fear.

tribunal, -alis, n., raised platform, tribunal.

tribuo, -ui, -utum (3), assign, give.

tribus, -us, f., tribe (division of the Roman people).

triduum -i, n., (a period of) three days.

triumphalis, -e, triumphal, one who has enjoyed a triumph.

triumpho (1), triumph, celebrate a triumph.

trucido (1), butcher, murder.

trux, trucis, wild, fierce.

tu, te, etc., you.

tueor (2), watch over, protect, defend.

tum, adv., then.

tumulus, -i, m., mound, hillock.

tumultuosus, -a, -um, confused, pell-mell.

tumultus, -us (4) (national) peril.

tunc, *adv.*, then.

turba, -ae, *f.*, rabble, mob, crowd.

turbulentus, -a, -um, wild, stormy.

turmatim, *adv.*, in squadrons (*of cavalry*).

tutor (1), guard, protect.

tutus, -a, -um, safe, secure ; in tutum, to safety (*Livy*).

tuus, -a, -um, your.

tyrannis, -idis, *f.*, despotism, tyranny.

tyrannus, -i, *m.*, tyrant, despot.

U

ubi, *interrog. and relat. adv.*, when, where.

ullus, -a, -um, any.

ultimus, -a, -um, further, most remote.

ultor, -oris, *m.*, avenger.

ultro, *adv.*, unasked, unsought, voluntarily.

ululatus, -us, *m.*, howling, war-whoop.

umerus, -i, *m.*, shoulder.

umquam, *adv.*, ever.

una, *adv.*, together.

undecimus, -a, -um, eleventh.

undique, *adv.*, from *or* on all sides.

universus, -a, -um, all, all together.

unquam, *adv.*, ever.

unus, -a, -um, one, alone, single.

urbs, urbis, *f.*, city.

usquam, *adv.*, anywhere.

ut *or* uti, *conj.*, as, when (*with indic.*) ; (*in order*) that, so that (*with subj.*).

uter, -tra, -trum, which (*of two*)?

uterque, -traque, -trumque, each of two, both ; utrique, *pl.*, each of two sides, both parties.

Utica, -ae, *f.*, Utica (*North Africa*).

Uticensis, -is, *m.*, citizen of Utica.

utilis, -e, useful, advantageous ; expedient (*Nepos*).

utique, *adv.*, in any case.

utor, usus (3), *with abl.*, use, make use of ; enjoy (*Nepos*).

utrum, *interrog. adv.*, whether.

uxor, -oris, *f.*, wife.

V

vacuus, -a, -um, empty, free, unoccupied ; (*of time*), free, disengaged (*Cicero*).

vado (3), stride.

vagor (1), wander, range.

vagus, -a, -um, straggling.

valeo (2), am strong, am well ; have weight (*Nepos*) ; prevail (*Caesar*).

vallum, -i, *n.*, rampart, wall, barrier.

varius, -a, -um, changing.

Varus, -i, *m.*, Varus.

-ve, *conj.*, or.

vehementer, *adv.*, hotly, strongly.

veho, vexi, vectum (3), carry ; in *pass.*, ride (*Cicero*).

Veii, -orum, *m.*, *pl.*, Veii (*town in Etruria*).

vel, *conj.*, or ; vel ... vel, either ... or.

vel, *adv.*, even, indeed.

velut, *adv.*, as if.

venerabundus, -a, -um, reverential, with respect.

venio, veni, ventum (4), come.

verbum, -i, *n.,* word; **verba facere,** to speak.

vere, *adv.,* truly, really.

vereor (2), fear, be afraid.

vero, *adv.,* in fact, indeed, however; even (*Cicero*).

verso (1), *in pass.,* to be, find oneself in; be engaged in (*Nepos*).

verto, -ti, -sum (3), turn.

verum, *adv.,* but.

verum, -i, *n.,* the truth, reality.

vesper, -eris *or* **eri,** *m.,* evening; **ad vesperum,** at evening.

vester, -tra, -trum, your.

Vestalis, -e, Vestal; *as noun,* a Vestal virgin.

vestibulum, -i, *n.,* entrance, vestibule.

vestimentum, -i, *n.,* dress, clothes.

vestio (4), clothe.

vestis, -is, *f.,* clothes, dress.

vexo (1), harass, disturb.

via, -ae, *f.,* way, street.

vicis, *acc.,* **vicem, in vicem,** in turn.

victor, -oris, *m.,* victorious.

victoria, -ae, *f.,* victory.

victrix, -icis, *f.,* victorious.

videlicet, *adv.,* it is plain, forsooth.

video, vidi, visum (2), see, observe; *in pass.,* seem, appear.

vigilia, -ae, *f.,* watch (*of the night*).

vilis, -e, cheap, worthless.

vincio, -nxi, -nctum (4), bind; **vinctus,** in chains.

vinco, vici, victum (3), conquer, defeat.

vinculum, -i, *n.,* chain.

vindico (1), punish (*Sallust*); avenge (*Livy*).

vinea, -ae, *f.,* mantlet.

vir, viri, *m.,* man, hero; husband.

viriditas, -tatis, *f.,* freshness.

virtus, -tutis, *f.,* courage, valour, merit.

vis, vim, *abl.,* **vi,** violence, force; quantity (*Caesar*); *in pl.,* **vires,** strength.

visus, -us, *m.,* seeing, sight.

vita, -ae, *f.,* life.

vivo, vixi, victum (3), live.

vivus, -a, -um, living, alive.

voco (1), call, invite.

vocula, -ae, *f.,* little voice.

volo, velle, volui, wish, willing.

voluntas, -tatis, *f.,* wish, desire.

volvo, -vi, volutum (3), ponder, reflect.

Volux, -ucis, *m.,* Volux (*son of Bocchus*).

vos, you.

vox, vocis, *f.,* (voice), saying.

vulgo *or* **volgo,** *adv.,* commonly.

vulnus, -eris, *n.,* wound.

vultus, -us, *m.,* face, look.